IN
AMERICAN
HISTORY

THE HOME FRONT DURING WORLD WAR II IN AMERICAN HISTORY

R. Conrad Stein

Enslow Publishers, Inc.

40 Industrial Road   PO Box 38
Box 398   Aldershot
Berkeley Heights, NJ 07922   Hants GU12 6BP
USA   UK

http://www.enslow.com

Library of Congress Cataloging-in-Publication Data

Stein, R. Conrad.
     The home front during World War II in American history /
R. Conrad Stein.
          p. cm. — (In American History)
Summary: Describes the experiences of those men and women who remained in
the United States during World War II, discussing their emotional ups and
downs, financial status, hard work, patriotism, fear, tension, shortages, and
loneliness.
     Includes bibliographical references (p.) and index.
     ISBN 0-7660-1984-5
     1. United States—History—1933–1945—Juvenile literature. 2.
United States—Social conditions—1933–1945—Juvenile literature. 3. World
War, 1939–1945—United States—Juvenile literature. 4. World War,
1939–1945—Social aspects—Juvenile literature. [1. World War,
1939–1945—United States. 2. United States—Social
conditions—1933–1945.] I. Title. II. Series.
E806 .S7834 2002
973.917—dc21
                                        2002005261

Printed in the United States of America

10 9 8 7 6 5 4 3 2 1

To Our Readers: We have done our best to make sure all Internet Addresses
in this book were active and appropriate when we went to press. However,
the author and the publisher have no control over and assume no liability
for the material available on those Internet sites or on other Web sites they
may link to. Any comments or suggestions can be sent by e-mail to
comments@enslow.com or to the address on the back cover.

Illustration Credits: Enslow Publishers, Inc., pp. 10, 26; Reproduced
from the Collections of the Library of Congress, p. 86; National Archives
and Records Administration, pp. 8, 11, 22, 24, 29, 33, 36, 38, 43, 45,
47, 52, 55, 56, 67, 68, 70, 71, 72, 88, 95, 97, 100.

Cover Illustration: National Archives and Records Administration.

★ CONTENTS ★

AN INCIDENT ON THE HOME FRONT

A bus crowded with factory workers rolled over the city streets. Speaking loudly, a woman told a fellow passenger, "Me and my husband are earning more money now than we ever have before, so I hope this war goes on for a good long while." Suddenly an older woman stood up and slapped her soundly in the face. With tears rolling down her cheeks, the older woman shouted, "That's for my son who's in the navy. I worry about him all the time. I can't even sleep nights." The woman who did the slapping then returned to her seat and broke into sobs. Other passengers sat in uneasy silence.

This incident on a bus is a true story. Versions of it appeared in newspapers and magazines late in 1942. At the time, the United States had been at war for a little less than one year. The slapping scene was a tiny episode in a grand drama that was popularly called the home front. The drama involved men, women, and children who remained at home during World War II. Many of them manufactured a miraculous amount of war material for use on the battlefields. That flood of material—guns, tanks, ships, airplanes, uniforms, radios, and thousands of other items big and small—paved the path to victory in World War II.

For Americans the home-front experience was one of intense emotional ups and downs. On the one hand, workers enjoyed full employment and had money in their pockets. These sudden riches stood in sharp contrast to the Great Depression of the 1930s. During the Depression years, one out of every four people suffered from joblessness and wretched poverty. The Depression was caused by a stock market crash that took place in 1929. On the other hand, home-front citizens agonized over family members or close friends serving in combat zones thousands of miles away.

Overriding all other emotions was a certainty that the United States was on the right side in this world conflict. World War II was, in the eyes of Americans, a just war. Citizens stood as one to achieve a single purpose: the defeat of an evil enemy. Home-front people realized that the cost of final victory would be high. Therefore, life in the United States was filled with fear, tension, shortages, loneliness, hard work, and patriotism. The home-front era was an experience like no other. And it began on a day that changed the world.

Japanese negotiations have come to practical stalemate. Hostilities may ensue. Subversive activities may be expected.[1]

—A message sent from Washington, D.C., to General Walter Short, the army commander of Hawaii on December 6, 1941.

REMEMBER PEARL HARBOR

The Day of Infamy

The day of December 7, 1941, dawned bright and sunny over the American military base at Pearl Harbor, Hawaii. It was Sunday, a day of rest for the soldiers and sailors. Many of them slept late. Others put on uniforms and prepared to go to church services. Just before eight in the morning, aircraft engines rumbled over the ocean. No one was alarmed. Surely they were American planes on maneuvers. Then, suddenly, a powerful explosion rocked the stillness of the Sunday morning. Men looked up to see the sky filled with planes. These were not American aircraft. A blazing sun, the symbol of the Japanese Empire, was painted on their wings.

Like angry dragonflies the Japanese planes swarmed down upon the giant battleships tied up at the harbor. This was the heart of the American fleet, a

Fire and smoke billowed up from the U.S. military base at Pearl Harbor, after a Japanese air raid took American forces by complete surprise.

formation called "Battleship Row." On board the *Nevada*, sailors were raising the flag, and a band was playing "The Star-Spangled Banner" when a plane ripped the deck with machine-gun fire. A torpedo dropped from another warplane and arrowed into the side of the *Oklahoma*, striking the ship with a roar of thunder.

The attack was a total surprise. At first no ship returned fire. The enemy flew so low that sailors saw the pilots' faces. Many Japanese pilots were grinning. A line of bombers dove toward the *Arizona*. Bombs tore through the *Arizona*'s deck and exploded deep inside the great ship. Nearby sailors later claimed the thirty-two thousand-ton battleship jumped a foot out of the water and then sank in a ball of flames.

Three minutes after the first bomb dropped, a frantic radio operator sent out the message: "AIR RAID, PEARL HARBOR—THIS IS NO DRILL."

Home television did not exist in 1941. Instead, families gathered around the living-room radio to listen to plays and musical programs. Millions of Americans were enjoying a CBS broadcast of the New York Philharmonic Orchestra when, at 3:00 P.M. eastern standard time, the music stopped. An announcer said, "We interrupt this broadcast to bring you a special announcement. . . ." A stunned silence gripped people in living rooms around the country as the radio voice claimed naval aircraft from Japan had bombed American ships at Pearl Harbor, Hawaii.

Shock! Anger! Disbelief! Some family groups dropped to their knees and prayed. Others looked at maps to determine where this Pearl Harbor place was. Hawaii at the time was an American territory, not a state, and Pearl Harbor was an obscure base. Millions of people in living rooms exploded into rage. More than half a century later, American men and women who lived through that day would still remember exactly where they were and what they were doing when they heard of the terrible air attack.

The next day President Franklin D. Roosevelt appeared before an emergency session of Congress. His speech was broadcast on radio, and a record

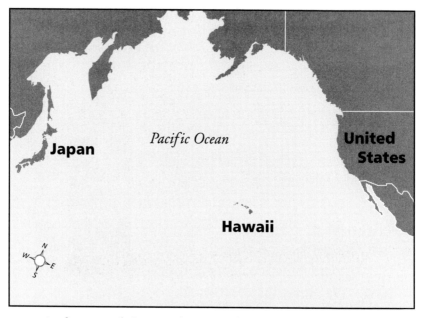

At the time of the attack on Pearl Harbor, Hawaii, many Americans did not know where the territory of Hawaii was.

audience of 60 million Americans listened. Carefully and coldly the president said, "Yesterday, December 7, 1941—a date which will live in infamy—the United States of America was suddenly and deliberately attacked by naval and air forces of the Empire of Japan."[2]

Roosevelt asked Congress for a declaration of war on Japan. After debating for less than one hour, Congress granted the declaration. Eighty-two members of the Senate unanimously voted for war, while the House of Representatives voted 388 to 1 in favor of the declaration. Three days later Germany and Italy declared war on the United States. Pearl

President Franklin D. Roosevelt signed a declaration of war against Japan on December 8, 1941. Three days later, Germany and Italy declared war on the United States.

Harbor—the Day of Infamy—had plunged America into the horrors of World War II.

The Winds of War

World War II was the bloodiest conflict in the human experience. Some fifty nations and more than half the world's population took part in the war. The devastating clash of arms lasted until 1945 and the exact number of people who died is uncertain. Some historians claim that up to 50 million people died because of the war, including both soldiers and civilians.

World War II grew out of the aftermath of World War I, which was fought between 1914 and 1918. Ironically, World War I was called "the war to end all wars." Germany was the principal defeated power in World War I. The defeat and subsequent reparations, or compensation for wrongdoing, that Germany had to pay to various nations left the German people bankrupt, confused, and without effective leadership. Into this chaos stepped the ex-army corporal, Adolf Hitler. A fiery speaker, Hitler blamed Jews and Communists for Germany's ills. (Communists believed in an economic system where all property was owned by the government, but shared by all the people.) Heading the Nazi Political party, Hitler took office in Germany in 1933. In violation of international treaties put in place after World War I, he began building up Germany's armed forces.

Hitler and the Nazis were guided by a political movement called fascism, which gained popularity in the wake of World War I. Fascism preached that the state was more important than the individual. The fascist Benito Mussolini rose to power in Italy, and fascists took over Spain as well. In the Soviet Union (which included present-day Russia) the communist Joseph Stalin became an iron-handed dictator. Complicating the political scene was the worldwide economic depression that struck in the early 1930s. Jobless people, desperate and starving, became willing followers of absolute rulers who promised to restore order and prosperity.

On September 1, 1939, Hitler shattered the uneasy peace in Europe by attacking Poland. Great Britain and France, allies with Poland, declared war on Germany. From the beginning, newspaper writers called this new European conflict World War II. The German Army waged a shocking form of warfare called *blitzkrieg*, meaning "lightning war" in German. Hitler's fast-moving tanks and airplanes electrified the world with quick conquests of Poland, Denmark, Norway, Belgium, and finally France. After France fell, only Great Britain stood alone against Hitler. In 1941 Hitler took an incredible gamble and attacked the giant nation of the Soviet Union.

Leaders in the United States viewed the fighting in Europe with alarm, but the nation remained neutral. Politicians divided into two feuding camps. The isolationists wanted to steer the country away from the European war, while others, including President Roosevelt, argued the United States should support England.

As the two camps bickered, a menacing situation had been developing in Asia. Japan was ruled by warlords who hoped to expand their nation's territory. In the 1930s, Japan began occupying land areas in China, and an undeclared war broke out between the two countries. The war was particularly brutal. Between 1936 and 1938, about 2 million Chinese civilians were killed. Japanese troops raped Chinese women and shot prisoners. Americans, reading about these atrocities, developed a hatred for Japan long before the attack on Pearl Harbor. To force the Japanese out of China, President Roosevelt refused to sell Japan essential goods such as iron, steel, and oil. This boycott infuriated the warlords. Hoping to break the back of the American Navy in one powerful attack, Japan launched its air raid on Pearl Harbor.

The Japanese came shockingly close to achieving their goal. When the smoke cleared at Pearl Harbor,

American forces counted their losses. Some twenty-four hundred American soldiers and sailors were killed. Seven of the fleet's eight battleships were either sunk or severely disabled. At least 188 American airplanes were destroyed, most of them while parked on the ground. It was the worst naval disaster in American history.

Despite the horrifying losses, the Japanese air raid planted the seeds of America's final victory. Isolationism died with the bombs that fell on the Pacific fleet. The Day of Infamy united the country as never before. For the next four years, the words "Remember Pearl Harbor" rang out as the nation's battle cry.

This war is diabolically different from all other wars. The pattern of [enemy] aggression reaches down into the homes of the countries that have been attacked—destroying them, reducing them to rubble, searing them with flame. . . . This is a civilians' war—and as civilians we must face the full fury of our enemies, who have no respect for an . . . unarmed opponent.[1]

—A memorandum issued by the New York State Council of Defense on March 13, 1942.

A Nation in the Grip of Fear

Walk, Don't Run

The opening months of World War II were a time of mortal fear on the home front. Bombing or even an enemy invasion of American soil seemed to be a grim possibility. These fears were strikingly real. Responsible leaders in government and the military believed the enemy would strike civilian targets within the country. The mayor of New York City, Fiorello La Guardia, warned, "The war will come right to our cities and residential districts. Never underestimate the strength, the cruelty of the enemy."[2]

In late December 1941, a sudden storm hit the Los Angeles area. Powerful thunderclaps rattled the windows of bungalow homes. People shouted, "Air raid!" Hundreds of Los Angeles residents rushed outside, expecting to see a formation of Japanese bombers. They saw nothing but dark clouds. In other parts of the country, citizens also searched the sky. It made no difference to nervous Americans that neither the Germans nor the Japanese had bombers with sufficient range to cross the oceans and return to their bases. After all, an enemy air raid on Hawaii was once thought to be impossible.

In various cities merchants strung tape over storefront windows to stop flying glass in the event of a nearby bomb explosion. Some store owners prided themselves on creating intricate checkerboard

SOURCE DOCUMENT

IN NO TIME AT ALL THE CIVILIANS GOT A TASTE OF WAR. AIR RAID ALARMS SHRIEKED ON BOTH COASTS. BIG CITIES BLACKED OUT, OR TRIED TO. THERE WERE DOZENS OF CASUALTIES, MOSTLY FROM AUTO ACCIDENTS ON THE DARKENED STREETS. . . . ON MONDAY NIGHT [DECEMBER 8, 1941] AIR RAID ALERTS STARTLED THE WEST COAST. ENEMY PLANES WERE REPORTED COMING IN OVER SAN FRANCISCO. SEARCHLIGHTS COULD NOT FIND THEM AND THEY DROPPED NO BOMBS.[3]

The shock of Pearl Harbor triggered a wave of bogus enemy bomber sightings. These false alarms brought the war to American front doors.

taped designs on their front windows. Workers piled sandbags against the outside walls of banks, government buildings, and telephone offices to diminish the effects of a bomb blast.

Air-raid drills were practiced with deadly seriousness in 1942. Hastily organized civil defense councils ran the air-raid practices. Signs were posted telling people to "WALK, DON'T RUN" to the nearest air-raid shelter in the event of an attack. School basements and solidly built warehouses were designated as shelters in most cities.

Night drills, called blackouts, were chilling experiences on the home front. During the blackouts, people were required to stay at home with their lights out or their curtains tightly drawn. Lights from the ground made perfect targets for enemy bombers. Each neighborhood had an air-raid warden, usually an older man who was a veteran of World War I. Wearing a special white helmet, the air-raid warden tramped the streets and shouted at any careless household that had left a light on during a blackout. Many wardens blew police whistles that they bought at a local store. Ironically, some of those whistles were stamped "Made in Japan."

A chorus of sirens announced the night practices. Initially the sirens were improvised, coming from police cars or fire trucks. Reading, Pennsylvania, employed car horns from a used car lot to signal an air-raid alert. Blackout conditions remained in force until sirens or a gravel-voiced air-raid warden gave the all-clear signal. Another form of drill, called the dimout, required household lights to be turned out, but streetlights were either dimmed or off. Home-front Americans participated in these exercises willingly and often with good humor. A Chicago air raid warden had three young sons who earned new nicknames: Blackout, Dimout, and All Clear.

Children had mixed reactions to the air-raid preparations. For younger kids, they were the stuff of nightmares. Eerie sirens wailed and small kids envisioned bombs screaming down on their rooftops. For older boys and girls the drills were dramas of high excitement. Boy Scouts were chosen as bicycle messengers and charged with delivering handwritten messages from one air-raid warden to another. Pedaling a bike, with no headlight due to blackout rules, made the scout feel like a young hero. Girls Scouts played roles as "casualties." Smearing their faces and arms with catsup to simulate blood, the girls sprawled over the city sidewalks and waited to be picked up by volunteer stretcher bearers.

Even farm towns in inland states such as Iowa and Nebraska participated in the air-raid practices. Certainly no enemy aircraft could reach those isolated towns, and they had no military value anyway. But no one really knew what kind of miraculous flying machines the Germans and the Japanese might possess. Preparations for air raids and even enemy invasions went on everywhere. In rural Wisconsin, the American Legion organized a small army of licensed deer hunters to take to the woods if their area was assaulted by paratroopers.

Along the Atlantic coast there was sound military reasoning behind blackouts and dimouts. At night German submarines, the menace of the Atlantic, lay off the coastal cities. Submarine captains peered through periscopes at lights cast from windows and neon signs. In this way submarine commanders were able to see passing ships against the background of city lights. Slow-moving freighters made perfect targets for torpedoes. Therefore cities on the eastern seaboard had to observe strict blackout or dimout regulations. New York City's famous street Broadway, the glimmering "Great White Way," turned off its lights for the duration of the war.

Through the first half of 1942 the Atlantic coast was a battleground as German submarines, or U-boats, sunk ship after ship. German sub commanders called this the "happy time" because they destroyed so many U.S. ships. People living in coastal regions heard explosions during the night. In daylight they saw wreckage, an oil slick, and perhaps the floating bodies of dead seamen. The U.S. Navy quickly roped off the beaches where debris from torpedoed ships floated. The navy did not wish to inform the German high command of their deadly successes. It took many months for the navy to learn to cope with the U-boats. During the course of the war German submarines sank four hundred merchant ships off the nation's east coast, costing the lives of some five thousand seamen.

The Enemy Within

On a dark night in May 1942, a German submarine edged up to a beach along Long Island. At the same time another submarine approached the coast of Florida. From both subs came teams of men who paddled small boats to shore. They were German saboteurs. Each spoke fluent English and had lived and worked in the United States at various times. The men carried American money, civilian clothes, and devilish explosive devices. One such device was a bomb hidden in a lump of coal no bigger than a grapefruit. If that disguised bomb were shoveled into a blast furnace along with a regular load of coal, the furnace would blow sky high. Such an explosion would destroy a multimillion-dollar power plant or steel factory.

Things went wrong for the saboteurs from the beginning of their operation. An alert Coast Guard sentry caught the Long Island group burying their boat in the sand. The FBI quickly rounded up the Florida band. One of those men was arrested in a tavern while spending his American money on beer.

As far as is known, this endeavor by eight rather clumsy German agents was the only organized enemy attempt to plant spies or saboteurs on American soil during the World War II years. However, home-front Americans, beset by war nerves, saw secret agents everywhere. A new person moving into a town was held in suspicion. This was especially true if the newcomer spoke in a foreign accent. Radio dramas told stories of heroic home-front citizens who caught enemy agents before they could do their sinister deeds. Government posters that hung in post offices warned people about careless talk that might be overheard by spies. Residents along the east coast were urged never to reveal anything they might know about ship movements. One poster said: "LOOSE LIPS MIGHT SINK SHIPS." Another poster showed a drowning sailor and underneath him the words: "SOMEONE TALKED!"

Early in the war the worries of home-front Americans were genuine. The country faced a cruel and a ruthless enemy, one that would readily engage in sabotage and terrorism if the opportunity presented itself. Seized in this grip of fear, the nation forgot its principles as a democracy and imprisoned its own citizens.

The Japanese Internment

"THIS MANAGEMENT POISONS BOTH RATS AND JAPS,"[4] read a sign on the window of a West Coast restaurant. The first line of a popular song that suddenly popped up on the nation's radios went, "You're a Sap, Mr. Jap." On January 29, 1942, Henry McLemore of the San Francisco *Examiner* wrote, "Why treat the Japs well here? . . . Let 'em be pinched, hurt, hungry and dead up against it. Personally I hate the Japanese, and that goes for all of them."[5]

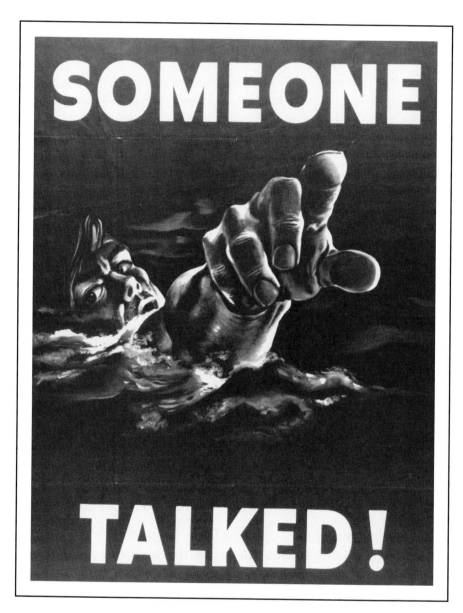

Posters warned Americans not to talk about sensitive wartime information like U.S. ship movements. Some believed that careless talk could be overheard by an enemy spy.

Pearl Harbor deepened a hatred of the Japanese that soon exploded into racism. California grocery stores refused to sell food to Japanese customers. Gas station operators declined to fill their tanks. Banks would not cash their checks. They were even turned away from churches. Loathing for everything associated with the new enemy spread throughout the country. The word "Jap" for Japanese was and still is considered a racial slur, an insult. After Pearl Harbor everyone—even teachers and preachers—used the word. The word appeared in headlines of respected newspapers and magazines.

In 1941 some one hundred ten thousand people of Japanese heritage lived along the West Coast. Fully seventy thousand of them were born on American soil. They were citizens by birth, and thereby entitled to equal protection under the law. Yet to most West Coast residents and to Americans in general, they were the despised Japs—untrustworthy, sneaky, and dishonest to the core. Worst of all, it was thought, every one of them was a spy for the empire of Japan.

In the wake of Pearl Harbor, rumors and stories of Japanese espionage circulated on the West Coast. It was said a Japanese gardener cut grass in such a way as to create an arrow pointing to a power plant. The gardener was thereby directing bombers from his nation. People claimed they saw Japanese residents signaling to submarines at night with flashlights. Japanese-American homes were rumored to have secret radios all tuned to Tokyo, the capital of Japan.

There was not a shred of evidence that any Japanese American who lived in the United States engaged in an act of disloyalty. But in the hysteria of war, the facts simply did not matter.

In February 1942, President Roosevelt signed the infamous Executive Order 9066. The order mandated the removal of people of Japanese heritage from coastal areas in California, Oregon, and Washington. "Why?" asked a Japanese citizen named Henry Murakami. "We hadn't done anything wrong. We obeyed the laws. None of us were spies."[6]

Families ordered to move were allowed to take only what they could carry. Hard-working Japanese had to give up their homes, their farms, their businesses, and their furniture. Evacuation was required for American-born citizens as well as for those born in Japan. "A Jap's a Jap," said General John DeWitt, who was in charge of

Executive Order 9066 ordered the removal of people of Japanese heritage from Pacific coastal areas. These children are being taken to internment camps in May 1942.

SOURCE DOCUMENT

THERE WAS NO PLACE I COULD GO TO BE COMPLETELY ALONE—NOT THE WASHROOM, THE LATRINE, THE SHOWER, OR MY STALL. . . . I COULDN'T AVOID THE PEOPLE I DIDN'T LIKE OR CHOOSE THOSE I WISHED TO BE NEAR. . . . IT WAS IMPOSSIBLE TO ESCAPE FROM THE CONSTANT NOISE AND HUMAN PRESENCE. I FELT STIFLED AND SUFFOCATED AND SOMETIMES WANTED TO SCREAM.[7]

Yoshiko Uchida was a Japanese-American college student living with her family in California when the war broke out. She and her family were interned in a camp to the west. In her book, Desert Exile, *Uchida describes the frustrations of camp life.*

defensive operations on the West Coast. "It makes no difference whether he's an American or not."[8]

Relocation camps for interned Japanese were built in inland areas, far from the Pacific coast. Much of this was desert land. Incoming families faced biting winds, freezing nights, and extremely hot days. By September 1942, some one hundred thousand Japanese had been put up in ten camps in seven western states. Dismal places, they consisted of cabins or tents enclosed by barbed-wire fences. A temporary camp in Puyallup, Washington, had one washroom with toilet facilities for every one hundred families. The camps were always surrounded by armed guards.

Even though they lived in miserable circumstances, the internees conducted a dignified life. They set up

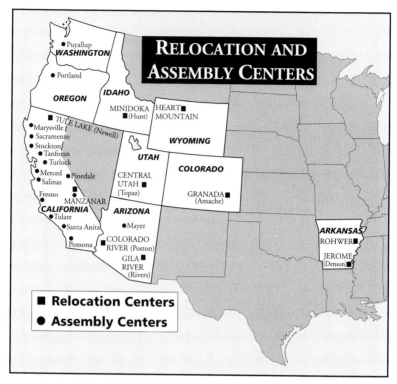

Japanese Americans were temporarily housed in assembly centers before they were shipped off to the more desolate relocation centers.

schools and all children attended classes. The internment lasted until 1944, and in that time, camp-run schools granted 7,220 high school diplomas. The people worked at farming and contributed to the war effort by sewing camouflage nets to be used on the battlefront. To the amazement of their guards, the internees started each day by raising the American flag, reciting the Pledge of Allegiance, and singing the National Anthem.

The United States was also at war with Germany and Italy. American authorities labeled some fourteen thousand German and Italian residents as possible security risks, and these people were detained and questioned. However they were interned on a case-by-case basis and only if authorities deemed them to be dangerous. The Japanese were allowed no such hearings. All were thought to be disloyal. Such was the rage the country felt over Pearl Harbor.

In spite of this shabby treatment, young Japanese men fought in the war and achieved an awesome combat record. The U.S. Army's 442nd Regiment consisted of eight thousand Japanese Americans, twelve hundred of whom signed up from the internment camps. Sent to Italy in 1943, the 442nd endured two years of almost constant combat and suffered an appalling number of casualties. The regiment won more medals for bravery than any other American unit its size in World War II. The men of the 442nd had a signature battle cry: "Go for broke!" They proved with their lives and their blood that Japanese people were loyal Americans.

4

THE WAR EFFORT

We are now in this war. We are all in it—all the way. Every single man, woman, and child is a partner in the most tremendous undertaking of our American history.[1]
—President Franklin Roosevelt, addressing the nation by radio on December 9, 1941.

Pearl Harbor presented the nation with a host of challenges. A huge army had to be raised. Factories had to be converted from the production of civilian goods to the manufacture of weapons. All the energies of the nation had to be channeled into what was called the war effort. Those two words—*war effort*—were heard dozens of times each day.

"Greetings"

In Portland, Oregon, a young man named Elliot Johnson ate lunch in a Chinese restaurant with three friends on December 7, 1941. "Suddenly the door of the kitchen burst open," said Johnson, "and the Chinese owner came running out, gesturing wildly . . . ."[2] Customers gathered around the restaurant's radio where they learned of Japan's attack on Pearl Harbor. Without finishing their meals, Johnson

Recruitment posters, such as this one for the U.S. Navy, urged men to serve their country by enlisting in the armed forces.

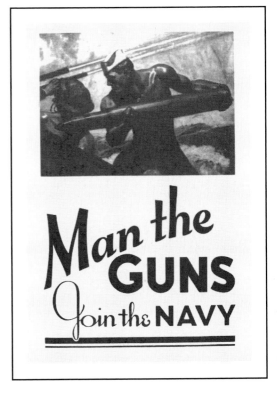

and his companions, ". . . got up and went directly to Marine head-quarters enlisting station. There was al-ready a line several blocks long."[3] And this on a Sunday when the young men knew the office would be closed.

In the weeks after Pearl Harbor, so many Americans tried to enlist in the army, navy, or marines (the air force at the time was a branch of the army), that the services could not process them fast enough. The urge to serve one's country affected young and old. In Detroit, Michigan, three generations—a grandfather, a father, and several sons—all lined up to join the army.

However not all men were so enthusiastic about enlisting. Many had families. Others had job skills that were desperately needed by the war effort. Hence came the draft and draft boards. The draft board organizations determined who would go to war and who would stay home. The military draft began in

1940, a year before Pearl Harbor. All men ages twenty-one to thirty-five were required to register at their local draft board. After the American declaration of war, the draft ages were expanded to eighteen and forty-five. Millions would receive letters: "Greetings: Having submitted yourself to a local board composed of your neighbors . . . you are hereby notified that you have been selected for training and service. . . ."[4]

Young men usually accepted their induction notices. Of the more than 10 million men ordered into the services, only about forty-three thousand refused to fight, for religious reasons. Those religious objectors were reviewed by draft boards and most were required to serve as medics, do farm work, or perform other noncombat duties. The vast majority reported for duty as ordered. Years later a typical draftee explained, "World War II was universally accepted by all of us who participated as a 'just war.' There was never any question of whether or not we were on the right side."[5]

Men drafted remained in the services for the duration of the war. *Duration*, meaning however long this war lasts, was another word often heard on the home front. If a store owner was drafted into the army, he might very well put up a sign on his storefront window stating, "DRAFTED, CLOSED FOR THE DURATION."

Most important, the draft system worked. In 1939, the United States had an army of three hundred seventy-five thousand men, seventeenth in size among the world's armies. Tiny countries such as Portugal and

SOURCE DOCUMENT

THE COFFEE THAT THEY GIVE US,
THEY SAY IS MIGHTY FINE,
IT'S GOOD FOR CUTS AND BRUISES
AND IT TASTES LIKE IODINE.
    CHORUS:
    I DON'T WANT NO MORE OF ARMY LIFE,
    GEE, BUT I WANT TO GO,
    GEE, BUT I WANT TO GO,
    GEE, BUT I WANT TO GO HOME.
THE BISCUITS THAT THEY GIVE US,
THEY SAY ARE MIGHTY FINE,
ONE FELL OFF THE TABLE
AND KILLED A PAL OF MINE. . . .[6]

Once they were in the army, American soldiers—as was true with soldiers from all nations—found plenty to complain about. Often their griping took a humorous note. This song, "Gee, But I Want To Go Home," was popular with civilians and soldiers alike. The chorus is belted out after every stanza.

Paraguay had more soldiers than the United States. By 1945 almost 16 million men and women served in either the army, the navy, or the marines in the United States. This massive military call-up was accomplished largely through the efforts of local draft boards.

Women were not subject to the military draft in World War II. Still, about two hundred sixty-five thousand women enlisted in women's auxiliary branches of the three services. At first the women were assigned "acceptable" tasks such as nursing and working as clerk typists. However, as the war dragged on, women became truck drivers and mechanics, jobs not open to them in peacetime. Almost two thousand women were trained as pilots. The female flyers were charged with the hazardous assignment of flying new and untested aircraft from factories to airfields around the country and to bases overseas. Women pilots achieved a better safety record than did the men. Still, thirty-eight female pilots were killed in crashes while doing their duties.

From Typewriters to Machine Guns

In early 1942 the last civilian automobile, a Ford, rolled off the assembly lines. At auto plants in Detroit a few workers lit candles and brought in flowers as if to mourn the final car. From now on, auto plants in the Motor City (a popular name for Detroit) and elsewhere would produce jeeps, army trucks, tanks, and aircraft.

Around the country other factories made conversions. A company that once manufactured typewriters changed its machinery and started churning out machine guns. Another plant went from making pots and frying pans to producing steel helmets for soldiers. A maker of rubber boots now made rubber rafts to serve as lifeboats on naval vessels. A firm specializing in wooden coffins shifted its efforts to fabricating wooden gliders for airborne troops.

Many factories switched to weapons production during wartime. Here, a female worker is surveying huge bombs, which were now being produced by the Firestone Tire and Rubber Company in Omaha, Nebraska.

Converting old factories to weapons production was only one element of the furious industrial mobilization that shook the nation at the start of the war. President Roosevelt called for the production of sixty thousand airplanes in 1942, and double that number the next year. These ambitious goals required the building of new industrial plants. In the first year of hostilities, $12 billion was spent on construction. Almost every dollar of that sum was used to build housing for servicepeople or to construct facilities for arms production. Some sixteen thousand new plants—large and small—were opened in 1942. Factories devoted to aircraft assembly zoomed from forty-one in 1940 to eighty-one in 1943.

The largest of the new industrial plants sprouting up was Willow Run, built near Detroit. When completed in 1942, the building was a half-mile long, a quarter mile wide, and served forty-six thousand workers. It was correctly described as "the biggest room in the world." Operated by the Ford Motor Company, Willow Run had one purpose: to build giant, four-engine B-24 bombers. At peak production, the plant was an industrial wonder. Raw steel, wire, and aluminum went into one end of the barnlike structure, and shiny new bombers came out of the other. Ford's engineering chief boasted of Willow Run, "Bring the Germans and Japs in to see it [and] they'll blow their brains out."[7]

The tanks, guns, and other war material produced by inland factories had to be shipped to the east and west coast ports for delivery overseas. In the 1940s the bulk of cargo was moved by train, not trucks. A decade of depression in the 1930s had weakened the nation's railroads. However the train system sprang to life with the start of the war. Some three thousand new locomotives and one hundred sixty-eight thousand new freight and passenger cars were built during the war years. In wartime it was common to see double and triple locomotives pulling a line of freight cars that stretched almost a mile long.

1942—Disappointments and Hope

Every morning home-front men and women read the newspapers and followed the progress of the war. They also got war news from radio broadcasts and newsreels they saw at the movies. In the first half of 1942, most of the stories coming from overseas told of disasters. In June, German troops seized the important port of Tobruk in North Africa. In September, Hitler's tanks rolled into the city of Stalingrad, deep in the heart of Russia. Meanwhile Japanese forces gobbled up territory in the Pacific. The British lost Hong Kong and Singapore. The worst blow to the United States came in April and May when the Japanese Army overwhelmed the Philippines and captured more than eleven thousand Americans. The Philippine defeat was one of the worst military reversals in U.S. history.

Home-front residents bore the setbacks of early 1942, with resolve. Most Americans had faith that their country would ultimately win this war. And, even during a year of crushing disappointments, there emerged a few signs of hope.

In April 1942, a group of sixteen B-25 bombers rumbled from the deck of the aircraft carrier *Hornet* and made a daring air raid on Japan. The bombers were led by Colonel James Doolittle, who awarded the Congressional Medal of Honor and became an instant hero. In June, American aircraft sank four Japanese carriers at the Battle of Midway. In August, U.S. Marines landed on the steamy tropical island of Guadalcanal to launch the first

A B-25 bomber takes off from the aircraft carrier Hornet *in April 1945. The aircraft participated in a raid over Japan which boosted home-front morale.*

ground offensive against Japan. On the other side of the world, Germany suffered a staggering defeat against Soviet soldiers in the ice and snow of Stalingrad. In November, American forces landed in North Africa and helped the British push the German and Italian armies off of that continent.

The year 1942 began as one of despair, but ended with promise. British Prime Minister Winston Churchill sounded a note of cautious optimism when he spoke of the Allies' advances in North Africa: "Now this is not the end. It is not even the beginning of the end. But it is, perhaps, the end of the beginning."[8]

THE ARSENAL OF DEMOCRACY

If 1942 was the time to build a war-making machine, 1943 was the year to get that machine rolling in high gear. Even before America's entry into World War II, President Roosevelt had promised to turn the United States into an "arsenal of democracy." After Pearl Harbor the American arsenal equipped its own armies and those of its allies. No nation on earth came even close to achieving the production miracles of the American home front.

From the Factories

In the 1940s, factory buildings were part of the make-up of industrial cities. Manufacturing centers such as Chicago boasted big, brooding factories that covered a city block and stood eight to ten stories tall. By 1943, those industrial plants were the living, throbbing heartbeat of the war effort. Three shifts of workers kept them alive twenty-four hours a day. At night, lights poured from the plants' windows while the pounding of punch presses and the whirl of drilling

Most wartime factories, like this aircraft plant in Nashville, Tennessee, stayed open twenty-four hours a day and employed three shifts of workers.

machines testified to the frenzied pace of work within the walls.

As the conflict progressed, American factories produced war material in staggering quantities. The rugged army vehicle called the jeep jumped off assembly lines at the rate of one every two minutes. In a typical month in 1943, the United States produced more light machine guns than did Japan in the entire course of the war. At war's end the arsenal of democracy had created 47 million tons of artillery shells, and 44 billion bullets for rifles and machine guns.

Factories in Germany doubled their output from 1940 to 1943, but that increase could not compare to production in the United States. By 1943, American industrial plants were churning out twenty-five times more goods than they did in 1940. Steel plants in 1943 produced twelve tons of raw steel for every American soldier. At the end of 1943 the United States had made twice as many weapons as had its combined enemies: Germany, Japan, and Italy.

The overflow from the United States' industrial plants supplied its principal allies, namely Great Britain and the Soviet Union. So many thousands of trucks arrived in the Soviet Union from the Studebaker Company of South Bend, Indiana, that the average Russian came to believe that the English word for truck was *Studebaker*. In 1943, the Russian premier Joseph Stalin met with Roosevelt and proposed a toast: "To American production, without which this war would have been lost."[1]

Between 1940 and 1945, home-front factories produced goods in numbers that were undreamed of before the war. Below is a partial list of material delivered by American industries to the fighting forces:

Tanks and self-propelled guns 102,000
Trucks 2,500,000
Artillery pieces .372,000
Aircraft 300,000

America's enemies simply could not match these amazing production figures. Much of World War II was a war of machines. Clearly, home-front workers won the machine-production aspect of the conflict.

SOURCE DOCUMENT

THE AXIS POWERS [GERMANY, JAPAN, AND ITALY] KNEW THAT THEY MUST WIN THIS WAR IN 1942—OR EVENTUALLY LOSE EVERYTHING. I DO NOT NEED TO TELL YOU THAT OUR ENEMIES DID *NOT* WIN THIS WAR IN 1942. WE KNOW THAT AS EACH DAY GOES BY, JAPANESE STRENGTH IN SHIPS AND PLANES IS GOING DOWN AND DOWN, AND AMERICAN STRENGTH IN SHIPS AND PLANES IS GOING UP AND UP. . . . I CAN REPORT TO YOU WITH GENUINE PRIDE ON WHAT HAS BEEN ACCOMPLISHED IN 1942. WE PRODUCED 48,000 MILITARY PLANES—MORE THAN THE AIRPLANE PRODUCTION OF GERMANY, ITALY AND JAPAN PUT TOGETHER. WE PRODUCED 56,000 COMBAT VEHICLES. WE PRODUCED 670,000 MACHINE GUNS. I THINK THE ARSENAL OF DEMOCRACY IS MAKING GOOD.[2]

President Roosevelt had called for the manufacture of sixty thousand airplanes in 1942, but home-front factories fell twelve thousand planes short of that goal. However, Roosevelt's State of the Union speech in January 1943 sounded much like a coach congratulating his team for a winning effort.

From the Shipyards

Of all the production miracles achieved by the home front, none was more incredible than the ship-building records. Between 1940 and 1945 American shipyards produced more vessels, large and small, than all the ships that were floating in all the seas of the world in 1935.

The workhorse of World War II cargo carriers was the Liberty Ship. During the course of the war more than twenty-seven hundred Liberties were assembled in American shipyards. Sluggish and clumsy-looking, Liberty Ships were about half a football field in length. They cruised at a speed of just over twelve miles an hour. Sailing vessels carrying cargo one hundred years earlier crossed the Atlantic faster than did a Liberty. Franklin Roosevelt, who admired the lines of classic naval ships, called the Liberties "ugly ducklings." Despite their ungainly appearance, Liberties were superb at moving freight. Their hulls could fit 300 freight cars, or 440 tanks, or 2,840 jeeps.

The greatest builder of Liberty Ships was the Kaiser Company with its main shipyard at Richmond, California. All Liberties were identical to each other. Therefore Kaiser developed the process of building huge sections of the ships in inland plants. The sections were then shipped by rail to be assembled like giant jigsaw puzzle pieces in coastal shipyards. In this way, Kaiser employees were able to cut the time of Liberty Ship production from two hundred days in 1941 to forty days in 1942. The corporation was owned by Henry Kaiser, a self-educated engineer who before the war knew nothing about building ships. Old-time navy men cringed when Kaiser referred to the ship's bow as its "front end," and its stern as the "rear end."

Battleships and aircraft carriers were the war's glamour ships. Thousands of workers swarmed into shipyards at Newport News, Virginia, each morning to build giant *Essex* class aircraft carriers. Holding ninety aircraft, the *Essex*-type ships led the fleet in the Pacific. Mightiest of all the battleships were the *Iowa* class vessels built between 1940 and 1944. These battlewagons displaced forty-five thousand tons and sported massive sixteen-inch-wide guns. Their launching was a cause of celebration on the home front. It was on the deck of one of these battleships—the *Missouri*—that the Japanese government signed the surrender agreement ending World War II.

Shipyards big and small contributed to the navy buildup. The Bethlehem Steel Company constructed shipyards on both coasts and increased its payroll from 7,000 to 210,000 employees. Ship-building activity was not confined to the coasts, however. The Lake Michigan town of Manitowoc, Wisconsin, expanded its ship-building plants and began to mass-produce submarines. In all, American builders assembled 5,425 cargo vessels and 87,000 warships and landing craft during the war years.

From the Farms

In 1940, four out of every ten Americans lived and worked in farming regions. The Great Depression of the 1930s caused crop prices to fall and plunged farming communities into poverty. The war invigorated American farms because the nation now had to feed its workers and its armies and send food to overseas allies. To ensure plentiful foodstuffs, the government offered farmers parities (guarantees) that paid them a set price for whatever they grew. In the past farmers had to

Here, the submarine Robalo *launches from shipyards in Manitowoc, Wisconsin, on May 9, 1943.*

accept whatever price they could get on the open market when they sold their crops. The parity system gave farmers a consistent income. Net cash income for farm families rose 400 percent from 1940 to 1945.

Farmers were also urged to mechanize. While it was impossible for a city-dweller to buy a new car, farmers were allowed to buy tractors. From 1940 to 1945 the number of tractors employed by American farmers rose by 50 percent. With more money coming in, farmers doubled their use of commercial fertilizers. Machines and fertilizers resulted in higher crop yields. Harvests were 25 percent greater in 1943 than they had been in 1940. By 1945, the average American farmer grew enough crops to feed his or her family plus thirteen other people.

These bountiful harvests came despite the fact that an estimated eight hundred thousand farm workers left the fields to take higher-paying jobs in factories. The field hands were replaced in part by workers from Mexico. A wartime measure called the *bracero* program allowed Mexicans to cross the border and help harvest U.S. crops. (The word *bracero* is often translated as "helping hand.") An estimated four hundred thousand braceros left their Mexican villages to work on farms primarily in Texas and California. Historians claim the massive postwar migration of Mexicans to the United States was triggered by the bracero program.

Home-front citizens also fed themselves with the aid of "victory gardens." A program of neighborhood gardening to boost the nation's output of food was launched during World War I. In World War II, the vegetable plots were called victory gardens because just about any practice designed to help the war effort bore the name "victory." City people who never gardened before now planted and weeded rows of tomatoes, cabbages, potatoes, radishes, corn, and squash. By 1943, roughly 20 million victory gardens were in operation, producing one third of the country's fresh vegetables.

The garden plots sprouted everywhere—in back-yards, in empty lots, and along railroad tracks. Portland, Oregon, had victory gardens on the grounds

"WE'RE JUST *MADE* FOR EACH OTHER... I WATER HIS VICTORY GARDEN, AND HE STAKES MY TOMATO PLANTS."

Cartoons, like this one, appeared in newspapers and magazines to stress the importance of victory gardens to the American public.

of the city zoo. In Chicago the inmates of Cook County Jail planted victory gardens on their exercise field. Chicago prisoners were allowed to grow anything except corn. Guards feared a convict could hide under tall corn stalks and engineer an escape.

Paying for It All

In 1939, the U.S. government spent $8.7 billion for all its programs. By 1945, the yearly national budget had zoomed to more than $100 billion. After more than four years of war, the government had spent more than $330 billion, mostly for military expenditures. This figure was greater than the total sum of all the annual U.S. budgets from 1789 to 1940.

How did the nation pay these staggering costs? To raise money the government made everyone—even the lowest-paid factory hand—pay income taxes. In the past only middle- and upper-income people were taxed. Workers who had never paid income taxes before suddenly found themselves on the tax rolls. To make sure everyone paid his or her share of taxes, companies were required to withhold a portion of every worker's weekly paycheck. Thus the system of withholding taxes was born. Workers learned a new term: *take-home pay*, meaning one's weekly paycheck minus the tax contribution. As every worker today knows, withholding tax remains with us in the twenty-first century. And the withholding tax system began as a "temporary" wartime measure.

Because people on the home front had plenty of work, money from income taxes rolled into the national treasury. Corporations also paid taxes on their profits. In addition the government put a special tax on luxury items such as jewelry. Still, taxes alone failed to raise enough money to pay for wartime expenses. Therefore the government called on Americans to loan it money in the form of war bonds.

"Any bonds today," sang Bugs Bunny in one of his wartime cartoons. War bonds were paper certificates that stood as proof that one had given money in the form of a loan to the government. Bonds were sold in post offices, schools, and at the candy counter in movie theaters. Companies urged employees to buy bonds to hasten victory.

The most common form of bond purchased by working-class families cost $18.75. After ten years from the date of purchase, the bondholder was able to redeem the bond and collect twenty-five dollars. President Roosevelt bought the very first war bond on May 1, 1942. Roosevelt's bond cost $375, and it would be worth $500 in ten years. Bonds came in more expensive denominations ranging up to ten thousand dollars. Children got bonds for their birthdays or as graduation gifts. Radio programs signed off at night with the announcer saying, "Bye bye and buy bonds."

Advertising for bond sales became intense during the "War Loan" drives. There were seven such drives between 1942 and

BUY BONDS AT YOUR NEAREST SKOURAS THEATRE!

WHAT D'YA MEAN— YOU AIN'T GONNA BUY NO BONDS!

During World War II, posters like this one urged Americans to buy war bonds and to help the U.S. government pay for wartime expenses.

1945, and all were patriotic extravaganzas. War heroes were taken from the front lines, paraded down city streets, and then given a microphone so they could urge people to buy bonds. During one War Loan Drive the gorgeous movie star Hedy Lamarr announced she would kiss any wealthy donor who bought $25,000 worth of bonds. One man contributed the $25,000, but fainted in anticipation before the starlet could give him his promised kiss. The comedian Jack Benny was famous for playing the violin badly as part of his skits. He offered his violin to anyone buying $1 million in war bonds. The violin was worth about $75, but it sold for $1 million an hour after the offer.

Aided by Hollywood glitz and glitter, the bond program succeeded magnificently. During the course of the war, Americans spent almost $157 billion on war bonds.

[I] *learned how to use an electric drill, how to do precise drilling, how to rivet. I hadn't seen anything like a rivet gun or an electric-drill motor before except in Buck Rogers funny books. That's the way they looked to me. But I was an eager learner, and I soon became an outstanding riveter.*[1]

AN ARMY OF WORKERS

—Winona Espinosa, a nineteen-year-old woman who moved from Colorado to San Diego in 1942 and became a war worker.

Workers for Victory

The Great Depression of the 1930s discouraged and demoralized American workers. Wages fell and everyone feared losing his or her job. Conditions gradually improved late in the decade, but even in 1939, 15 percent of the workforce was unemployed. Then came Pearl Harbor. Unemployment vanished, and suddenly companies were crying for help. One shipyard worker remembered,

> Going to work in the navy yard, I felt like something had come down from heaven. I went from forty cents an hour to a dollar an hour. . . . At the end of the war I was making two seventy-five. I couldn't believe my good fortune. . . . We hardly ever went to the

picture shows during the Depression; now I did it all the time.[2]

The nation had about 186,000 factories in the early 1940s. As the conflict heated up they were called war plants, and they hummed with furious activity. Typically, war plants stayed open twenty-four hours and employed three shifts of workers. The first shift worked from 8:00 in the morning to 5:00 in the afternoon. The second shift arrived at 4:00 in the afternoon and worked until midnight. The third shift (nicknamed the "graveyard shift") toiled from midnight until 8:00 in the morning. This way the huge machines within the factory buildings kept pounding and churning out goods for victory.

Factory hands on the home front worked Saturdays and were often asked to work overtime; that is, beyond the customary eight-hour day. This wealth of work delighted jobholders who had suffered through the Great Depression. By law an employee received time-and-a-half wages for work beyond forty hours a week. A fifty-hour workweek was common in wartime. Before the war full-time employees were lucky to work thirty-seven hours. For the first time ever, unskilled workers reaped rewards. Average wages rose from $.73 an hour in 1941 to $1.02 in 1945. Weekly pay, with overtime wages, almost doubled. By 1945, family incomes of the lowest fifth had grown by almost 70 percent.

Industrial work was hard, grueling, monotonous, and often unsafe. A punch press operator, for example, spent all day sitting in front of a machine. The operator placed metal parts on a form, pushed a foot pedal that sent a punch crashing down on the part, and then removed the finished part to replace it with another. Punch press machines were frightfully noisy and the parts an operator fed into it were coated with grease. Working the punch press was an exercise in boredom. Every operation, each movement of the hands, was the same as the previous one. Yet if a worker's thoughts wandered for a second, he or she could lose a finger in the jaws of the powerful machine.

Most factory workers produced only parts—screws, springs, gears, brackets—that went into engines that in turn propelled tanks or aircraft. Top bosses nagged the floor bosses to keep the parts coming. Floor bosses, in turn, harassed the workers. Factory hands had a quota, a certain number of parts they had to produce during a shift. Workers who failed to meet their quotas were accused of being unpatriotic. Simply leaving one's machine to go to the bathroom was considered a shameful act. Hanging on the wall of some factory bathrooms was a sign bearing a picture of Adolf Hitler. Sporting an evil smile, Hitler says, "Take your time in here. You've got all day."

Without question workers and labor unions supported the war effort. But this loyalty left labor unions with a tricky question: How do they fight a company they believe is paying workers an unfair wage scale? Historically labor unions would call a strike and order workers to walk off their jobs, causing a

Staying home from work for any reason other than terrible illness was also considered an unpatriotic act, as illustrated in this wartime poster.

company or an entire industry to shut down. Now—in the middle of a desperate war—did such a shutdown aid the enemy?

Almost all major unions announced a no-strike pledge that held true through the course of the conflict. However, there were exceptions to labor's no-strike policy. In 1943, the fiery labor leader John L. Lewis called for a strike of the nation's coal miners. Coal was vital to the steel industry and therefore essential for the war effort. Immediately, Lewis became the most hated man in America. The army's official newspaper, the *Stars and Stripes*, said in an editorial, "John L. Lewis, damn your coal-black soul."[3] Luckily for the nation, the very messy coal strike was settled quickly and labor peace returned to the home front.

Because of wartime pressure, a wealth of jobs opened for disabled people, who had long been denied meaningful work. Deaf workers were sent to toil in the noisiest wards of factories or shipyards because they were not bothered by the terrible clamor of the machines. Blind men and women were given assembly-line assignments such as screwing metal pieces together. People of short stature crawled into the tiny corners of aircraft bodies to secure rivets. Disabled workers astounded their bosses with their production and their ability to learn new and challenging skills. Sadly, after the war, the disabled were the first to be dismissed. Once more it became difficult for a handicapped person to find work.

Women at Work

"A woman's place is in the home," went an old saying. When World War II began, three out of every four women of working age were housewives. They kept the home spotless, had a hot dinner on the table when their husband returned from work, and tended to the kids' every need. Pearl Harbor altered this pattern. The husband was now in the army or he had to work ten- to twelve-hour shifts. Businesses were crying for help. So women left the house and helped to win the war.

Wartime pressures allowed women to take jobs they had not dreamed of obtaining in peacetime. Women bus drivers and truck drivers navigated the streets. Women mechanics and tool makers worked in war plants. Women employees in the aircraft industry

SOURCE DOCUMENT

JUST A LITTLE OVER 2 YEARS AGO THE SUBJECT AND PURPOSE OF THIS BULLETIN WOULD HAVE BEEN CONSIDERED AS FANCIFUL AS A TALE FROM THE ARABIAN NIGHTS. THAT AMERICAN WOMEN SHOULD TAKE AN ACTIVE PART IN THE MAN'S JOB OF BUILDING AND REPAIRING SHIPS WAS ALMOST INCONCEIVABLE. . . . TIMES HAVE CHANGED WITH LIGHTNING SPEED. BY LATE 1943, THOUSANDS OF WOMEN ALONG BOTH COASTS AND ON THE GULF, GREAT LAKES, AND INLAND WATERWAYS WERE ACTIVELY ENGAGED IN ALMOST EVERY STAGE OF SHIP BUILDING AND REPAIR WORK, AND IT IS ANTICIPATED THAT IT WILL BE NECESSARY TO RECRUIT THOUSANDS MORE BEFORE THE WAR IS OVER.[4]

In 1944, Dorothy K. Newman, a sociologist in the Woman's Bureau in Washington, D.C., reported on the status of female workers in the nation's shipyards.

increased from four thousand in 1940 to three hundred sixty thousand in 1945. In ammunition plants, two out of every five workers were women. By 1945, women comprised 36 percent of the American workforce.

The symbol of American industrial might became not a man holding a wrench, but "Rosie the Riveter." On posters Rosie was pictured dressed in coveralls and defiantly flexing a muscle. With a determined look on her face, she says, "We Can Do It!" Popular memory holds that Rosie was a shipyard worker because shipbuilders employed almost 30 percent females. But female workers, which Rosie symbolized, were everywhere. The war could not have been won

like outsiders, people to be shunned. In 1944 a noted sociologist wrote, "War-working families live in war communities as strangers, objects of a rather pervasive social isolation. . . . This problem is real, serious, tragic."[6]

Still, endless rivers of workers poured into shipyard centers such as Mobile, Alabama; Hampton Roads, Virginia; and San Diego, California. A housing shortage plagued the boomtowns. New slums, or poor neighborhoods, developed. Writing from Mobile, Alabama, a reporter noted, "In cluttered backyards people camp out in tents and chickenhouses and shelters tacked together out of packing cases."[7]

The nationwide housing shortage lasted the duration of the war. Owners of rooming houses near aircraft plants rented what were called hot beds to factory employees. When one worker rose to report to the plant, the owner quickly changed sheets and gave the hot bed to another war worker coming off a shift. More than three hundred thousand newcomers swarmed into Washington, D.C., to take jobs as clerks. Housing became so scarce in the nation's capital that hotels limited guests to stays of only three nights. Sometimes a Washington office clerk went to work in the morning not knowing where he or she would sleep that night.

The Dilemma Facing African Americans

African Americans on the home front confronted a problem within a problem. First, their country fought the most vile racist power on earth in Nazi Germany. Second, the United States of the 1940s was itself a racist society. During World War II, African Americans served in segregated units of the armed forces. In southern states African Americans could not enter most restaurants, and they had to ride on the back seats of buses. Even bomb shelters in the South were marked "whites only" and "colored only." The situation was only slightly better in the North. Housing was segregated in northern cities. Newly arriving African Americans were forced to live in already overcrowded slums. African-American factory workers were generally given menial jobs and were denied training.

The home front during World War II was a time of unity. It was a rare period in history where Americans marched together to the beat of a single drummer. Yet it was also a time when African Americans grew frustrated over their position at the back of the parade. While the vast majority of black men and women worked for victory, they also demanded their share of the wartime prosperity enjoyed by white America.

One black leader who confronted white society was A. Philip Randolph, the influential head of the Sleeping Car Porters Union. Early in the war, Randolph demanded all war plants open their doors to African-American employees. When President Roosevelt was reluctant to issue such an order, Randolph threatened to gather thousands of his followers and stage a march on Washington. Such a march would destroy the image of home-front unity, and perhaps be used for propaganda by the nation's enemies. The president gave in and issued Executive Order 8802, which stated, "There shall be no discrimination in the employment of workers in defense industries or government because of race, creed color, or national origin."[8] Randolph had won a major victory, but enforcement of the president's order was spotty at best. Many smaller shops refused to hire African Americans despite the new law. Meanwhile, anger and frustration simmered in African-American communities.

Tensions were high in Detroit, Michigan, where fifty thousand African Americans had recently arrived from the South to take factory jobs. With decent housing closed to them, the African Americans were boxed into a slum called, ironically, Paradise Valley. On June 20, 1943, black and white teenagers got into a fight at a nearby city park. The fighting escalated. Rumors, which proved to be false, swept the black community that white mobs had killed three blacks. Blacks retaliated by pulling whites off streetcars and beating them savagely. Gangs of whites counterattacked. Soldiers and federal troops were sent into Detroit. By the time order was restored, twenty-five blacks and nine whites had been killed. *Time* magazine reported, "After 24 nightmarish hours, Detroit was quieted down, [and officials] counted the toll of one of the worst riots in modern U.S. history."[9]

Racial violence spread from Detroit to other cities in the steaming summer of 1943. Riots broke out in

Springfield, Massachusetts, and El Paso, Texas. In all, racial conflicts rocked forty-seven American cities. New York City's Harlem neighborhood, the unofficial capital of black America, exploded in August. The nationwide series of riots was an ugly scar on the home front period.

Despite all this turmoil, African Americans made genuine progress during World War II. Before the war, three out of every four African Americans lived in the South, where they were the poorest residents in the nation's poorest region. In southern farming communities, many African Americans lived under conditions that had barely improved since the days of slavery. Then, in the war years, some 2 million industrial jobs opened to African Americans. About 1.5 million African Americans moved to northern states and to California. The federal government hired two hundred thousand African Americans for civil service work.

Most important, African-American servicemen and servicewomen returned from the war vowing to dismantle the American system of segregation. For generations that system had made African Americans second-class citizens in the country of their birth. In many ways, the World War II experience served as the foundation for the civil rights revolution that swept the nation in the 1950s and 1960s.

V IS FOR VICTORY

The war ruled culture, entertainment, and everyday life on the home front. No one could escape wartime frenzy. Posters prodding people to work harder or to buy bonds hung everywhere. Wartime movies contained as much propaganda as they did plot. Shortages of food, housing, and gasoline plagued home-front citizens. Yet people worked together and managed to enjoy life. The nation's suicide rate actually decreased by 30 percent during the war years. Decades later Americans who did not lose loved ones in the war remembered the home-front years as some of the most fun-filled times of their lives.

The Big Letter V

Symbols were seen in every home-front city and town. A smiling Uncle Sam, the symbol of national pride, appeared on posters in post office buildings and in schoolrooms. Near Uncle Sam was the sinister picture of Hitler, the symbol of the hated enemy. Words beneath Hitler's picture warned people to work hard for victory or face a life of slavery under enemy

THIS IS A V-HOME!

WE IN THIS HOME ARE FIGHTING. WE KNOW THIS WAR WILL BE EASY TO LOSE AND HARD TO WIN. WE MEAN TO WIN IT. ... WE SERVE NOTICE TO ALL THAT WE ARE PERSONALLY CARRYING THE FIGHT TO THE ENEMY, IN THESE WAYS:

I. *THIS HOME FOLLOWS THE INSTRUCTIONS OF ITS AIR-RAID WARDEN*, IN ORDER TO PROTECT ITSELF AGAINST ATTACK BY AIR.

II. THIS HOME *CONSERVES* FOOD, CLOTHING, TRANSPORTATION, AND HEALTH, IN ORDER TO HASTEN AN INCREASING FLOW OF WAR MATERIALS TO OUR MEN AT THE FRONT.

III. THIS HOME *SALVAGES* ESSENTIAL MATERIALS, IN ORDER THAT THEY MAY BE CONVERTED TO IMMEDIATE WAR USES.

IV. THIS HOME *REFUSES TO SPREAD RUMORS* DESIGNED TO DIVIDE OUR NATION.

V. THIS HOME *BUYS* WAR SAVINGS STAMPS AND BONDS *REGULARLY*. WE ARE DOING THESE THINGS BECAUSE WE KNOW WE MUST *TO WIN THIS WAR*.[1]

A government paper written in 1942 spelled out the requirements for families to establish a "V-Home." The nation's leaders urged families to take this pledge.

dictators. By far the most pervasive wartime symbol was the capital letter *V*, meaning *V* for *Victory*.

Even baby brothers and sisters on the home front knew that dot-dot-dot-dash was Morse Code language for the letter *V*. Radio programs began with an orchestra blaring out: "dit-dit-dit-daah," which were also the opening notes of Beethoven's Fifth Symphony. Of course, announcers never reminded radio audiences that the great composer Ludwig van Beethoven was German. On windless days skywriting airplanes soared above cities and drew a giant letter *V* with a dot-dot-dot-dash below. Kids were awestruck by this aerial artwork.

The word *Victory* was attached to scores of items and concepts. Write a letter to a friend in the armed forces and you sent it via Victory Mail, or V-Mail. Tending a victory garden was one's patriotic duty. African Americans printed up posters with a double *V*, symbolizing victory over the foreign enemy and victory over racial segregation at home. War bonds were often called victory bonds. Sometimes the word was shamelessly exploited by advertisers. Certain companies self-proclaimed their products "Victory Cigarettes" or "Victory Beer."

Don't You Know There's a War On?

What caused excitement in a neighborhood on the home front? Many things. Perhaps a local boy who was wounded in action was coming home a hero. Communities regularly held block parties to honor their returning servicemen. Perhaps the Boy Scout troop or the high school band and marching corps were due to stage a victory parade down Main Street. All these events aroused a community. But true excitement came when the whispered word was passed from household to household, "Hey, Mrs. Wisnowski just got a shipment of toilet paper at her store." Then everyone rushed to the store to try to buy a few rolls before the supply ran out.

Shortages of household supplies frustrated home-front life. People had money in their pockets to buy goods, but store shelves were bare because consumer items were absorbed by the war effort. Goods in short supply included meat, butter, sugar, paper products, tires, shoes, and a host of other wares. Exasperated customers often complained to store owners about the shortages. To answer customer complaints, the owners uttered a famous wartime expression, "Don't you know there's a war on?"

The government attempted to ease the pain of shortages by rationing certain key items. Rationing meant everyone—rich or poor—had to bear an equal burden of scarcity. Thus began the complicated system of points and ration books, the scourge of home-front consumers. Large supermarkets were rare at the time. More common were small grocery shops, many of which were owned by women. Store owners as well as customers almost went crazy trying to figure out the baffling stamp book arrangement.

During World War II, shortages of certain household items, like sugar, often frustrated shoppers.

Based on its size, every American family was given books of color-coded ration stamps. The stamps had to be used along with cash when buying items at a store. Each stamp represented so many "points." To buy a pound of ground beef required 7 points, a can of sardines 12 points, a bottle of catsup 15 points, and so on. A pound of butter was a whopping 16 points. With people earning more than they ever had before, cash became a secondary consideration at the grocery store. For many families ration stamps were more important than money.

Some items such as butter and toilet paper disappeared from store shelves for weeks at a time. When

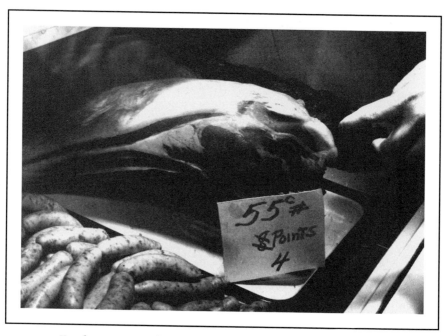

Food rationing during World War II gave rise to the complicated point system that labeled items in both their cash price and their value in "points."

these goods were in stock, store owners tried to preserve them for their best customers. Therefore the owners became "stoopers." A typical stooper hid precious goods from casual customers. But when a prized customer entered the door, the owner would stoop below the counter to retrieve the items.

Clothing was rationed along with food. One of the first items to disappear was women's nylon hosiery. Nylon was needed to make parachutes. Without nylon stockings, women painted their legs with a tan dye before going to a dance. Men wore "victory suits," without pants cuffs so as to conserve cloth. Shoes were rationed at the rate of two pairs per year per person. Parents frequently walked with holes in their soles so they could use precious ration coupons to buy new shoes for growing children. Even wealthy families were compelled to patch up old clothes and have their shoes resoled. The government wrote a snappy jingle to advise home-front citizens on how to stretch out their wartime wardrobes: "Use it up, wear it out/Make it do, or do without."[2]

Wartime travel meant a crush of people at train stations. Railroads carried some 90 percent of travelers in the 1940s. More than 2 million servicemen a month rode to and from bases or home on furlough. (A furlough is a break from military service.) Little room was left for civilians. Passengers were forced to stand or to sit on their suitcases overnight during long trips. The government pleaded with people to curtail leisure travel. Nagging signs at the train stations asked: "Is This Trip Necessary?"

The supply of home appliances dried up. If the refrigerator broke down, a family was hard pressed to buy a new one. "Fix-it" shops sprang up in storefronts. The shops were often run by elderly men who looked as if they needed a bath and a shave. Despite their unkempt appearance, the shopkeepers were geniuses in repairing small machines. If a vacuum cleaner or a toaster broke, its owner took it to the fix-it shop down the block. Perhaps an appliance needed a part that was unavailable. No problem. The old fix-it shop

Americans were cautioned against casual travel during the war. This cartoon expressed the frequently asked question: "Is this trip necessary?"

proprietor knew how to make new parts seemingly out of the air.

Though Americans complained about the shortages, they were the best-fed, best-dressed people in the world. A black market, which allowed people to buy rationed goods without using stamps, did exist. But the majority of people believed the black market was unpatriotic and shunned its use. However, there was one substance that proved to be the most irritating home-front shortage—gasoline.

Americans loved to drive because it was such a great convenience. So gas rationing was painful. Car

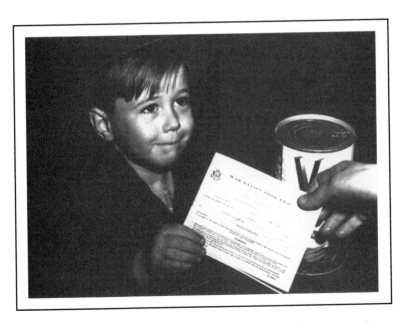

During the war, Americans were able to buy rationed goods on the black market, but this was considered unpatriotic. Most Americans, like this young boy, chose to purchase goods using the food ration book issued to them by the government.

owners were issued windshield stickers with large letters running from *A* to *E*. An *A* sticker meant that the government determined the owner did not need his or her car for work and was allowed only three gallons of gas a week. A *B* sticker was allotted more fuel. An *E* sticker, often given to doctors who made house calls, meant the owner could buy an almost unlimited supply of gasoline. From the beginning, a howl of protest went up over the gas rationing system. When gasoline was available through the black market, many Americans—including the patriots—bought the illegal fuel.

A critical shortage of rubber during the war years rationed the sale of tires and limited driving.

Curiously, there was no real shortage of gasoline in the United States. Gas rationing was imposed in order to save a seriously critical substance: rubber. In 1942 the Japanese conquered the East Indies and Malaya. Before the war, the East Indies and Malaya gave the United States upwards of 90 percent of its crude rubber supply. It was not until late in the war that American plants began to produce large quantities of synthetic rubber for military vehicles. To preserve rubber, the government imposed a "victory speed" of thirty-five miles per hour.

Because of gas rationing and the scarcity of rubber, traffic diminished sharply. Residential neighborhoods became almost eerily silent. Dogs roamed about freely. City boys played touch football on side streets and rarely had to interrupt their game to allow for the passage of a car. In rural areas weeds sprouted from cracks in the pavement. The United States—once a nation on wheels—became a country whose people walked on foot.

No Shortage of Entertainment

> Well, Los Angeles had its first blackout the other day. Every electric light in the city went out. I saw one guy standing in the street and laughing like anything. I said, "What are you so happy about?" And he said, "At last I'm not alone. Look—this month, nobody paid their bills."[3]

So quipped the comedian Bob Hope during his weekly radio show early in 1942.

The lively world of entertainment broke wartime tension. Comedians and musicians sought to please a people who were hardworking, fearful, and hungry to laugh.

In those pretelevision days, the average American listened to radio about four hours a day. At night family groups gathered around the living-room radio, staring at the glowing dial as if they saw pictures there. A situation comedy featuring a couple, called *Fibber McGee and Molly*, was ranked number one in popularity. The husband, Fibber, had arguments with his friendly air-raid warden. Few civilians missed the *Jack Benny Show*, a weekly comedy act. The war bled into comedy routines, as can be seen in this exchange between Jack Benny and his sidekick Dennis Day:

> **DENNIS**: You know, Mr. Benny, when I'm in the Navy, I hope people won't think I'm dumb . . . I took a [navy] intelligence test, and I got a mark of one hundred fifty-eight.
>
> **JACK**: One hundred fifty-eight?
>
> **DENNIS**: Sure, here's the card.
>
> **JACK**: *Dennis, this is your weight* . . . You *weigh* one hundred and fifty-eight pounds.
>
> **DENNIS**: Oh.[4]

Popular songs celebrated heroes in uniform: "Comin' in on a Wing and a Prayer," "Bell Bottom Trousers, Coat of Navy Blue," and "Boogie-Woogie Bugle Boy of Company B." Other tunes contained messages from faraway soldiers and had a "wait for me" theme: "Don't Sit under the Apple Tree with Anyone Else But Me," and "You'll Never Know Just How Much I Miss You." Conversely, home-front girls complained through songs that all the decent men were in the services, and as for those remaining at home: "They're Either Too Young or Too Old." Some songs poked fun at wartime shortages: "You Get No Bread with One Meatball." Many popular numbers were purely whimsical and were enjoyed for their nonsense meanings: "Mares Eat Oats and Does Eat Oats and Little Lambs Eat Ivy."

Broadway musicals paid tribute to the nation's soldiers, sailors, and marines. *On the Town* was a song-and-dance fantasy that followed the antics of three sailors on liberty, a break from service, in New York City. The hit 1943 musical *Something for the Boys* employed a glee club of servicemen and an official Army Air Force band. Most popular of all was Irving Berlin's lively *This Is the Army*. Boasting an all-soldier cast, *This Is the Army* earned forty thousand dollars a week for the Army Relief Organization.

Major-league baseball was the prime spectator sport in the 1940s. The game faced a crisis when baseball heroes such as Joe DiMaggio, Bob Feller, Ted Williams, Hank Greenberg, and others joined the services. With so many star players in uniform, the commissioner of baseball considered canceling the games for the duration of the war. President Roosevelt intervened, claiming baseball was required to maintain civilian morale. This meant teams had to make do with the players on hand. The Cincinnati Reds hired a sixteen-year-old pitcher, Joe Nuxhall, who had appeared in one game in 1944. The St. Louis Browns employed an outfielder named Pete Gray, who had lost his arm in a childhood accident. Gray served as an inspiration to the thousands of servicemen who were returning home minus an arm or a leg due to war injuries. Home-front fans cheered Gray's every turn at bat.

Women's baseball enjoyed a surge of popularity during World War II. As women took over men's jobs in the factories and shipyards, they also replaced men on the baseball diamonds. In 1943, an organization called the All-American Girls Baseball League (AAGBL) was formed. Most AAGBL teams represented midsized towns. All the players were women, but the teams were usually coached by men. Crowds came out to cheer squads such as the Muskegon, Michigan, Lassies or the South Bend, Indiana, Blue Sox. The AAGBL was so popular that it survived the war and did not disband until 1954.

Hollywood Goes to War

In 1943, moviegoers crowded into theaters to see the latest Tarzan adventure picture, *Tarzan Triumphs*. Normally these jungle epics were not connected to current events. But this was wartime. In the movie, Nazis have taken over an African village. The village queen appeals to Tarzan for help. Tarzan the Ape Man declines. "Nazi [will] go away," says Johnny Weissmuller, playing Tarzan. "You don't know them," snaps the queen. "Once they conquer us, they will spoil everything you stand for." Then the Nazis kidnap Boy, Tarzan's adopted son. Dramatically Tarzan draws his knife and declares, "Now Tarzan make war."[5] In theaters around the country audiences stood and cheered.

Between 1942 and 1945 Hollywood moviemakers shot seventeen hundred films, and at least five hundred of them were related to the war. Movies were by far America's most popular form of entertainment. Theaters in boomtowns stayed open twenty-four hours a day so workers coming off factory shifts could take in the latest Hollywood offering. Typically a movie house showed two films. Cartoons and a newsreel were shown in the middle of the double feature. Theaters changed pictures two or even three times each week to accommodate a movie-hungry audience.

The history of World War II can be traced through Hollywood's wartime movies. Early pictures such as *Wake Island* (1942) and *Bataan* (1943) showed American servicemen heroic in defeat. The tone of the movies shifted later in the war as U.S. forces took the offensive. *The Story of GI Joe* (1945) and *A Walk in the Sun* (1945) depicted American soldiers storming through Europe on the road to victory over Germany. *Back to Bataan* (1945) dramatized triumph over the Japanese on the Philippine Islands.

Propaganda messages were heavy-handed in many wartime films. German soldiers were portrayed as mindless robots, indifferent to the cruelties and suffering they imposed on innocent people. The 1943 film *Hitler's Children* gave American audiences a shocking study of how the Nazis trained their youth. Hollywood pictured Japanese fighting men as savages who lusted for war and conquest. The hate-the-enemy theme was particularly strong in the 1944 movie *The Purple Heart*. The film follows a U.S. bomber crew shot down after bombing Tokyo and subject to brutal interrogation and torture. Finally the crew members are marched off to be executed. The American pilot portrayed by actor Dana Andrews shouts to the Japanese officers, "This is your war—you wanted it. . . . and now you're going to get it—and it won't be finished until your dirty little empire is wiped off the face of the earth."[6]

Some movies drew upon home-front life. *Since You Went Away* (1944) dramatized the life of a wartime family. The father in the film served overseas while the mother and children lived in dread of getting a telegram from the War Department. Comedies broke the tension of home-front struggles. In *Blondie for Victory* (1942), the bungling husband, Dagwood, endured zany mishaps as his wife, Blondie, organized neighborhood women to pitch in for the war effort. A love comedy called *Swing Shift Maisie* (1943) told of the rivalry between two female aircraft assemblers competing for the attention of a handsome test pilot.

About fifteen thousand movie houses operated throughout the country in the war years. City neighborhoods had a theater every few blocks. Adult fare in local houses was about a quarter and children got in for as low as twelve cents. With theaters available and affordable, two out of every three Americans went to the movies at least once a week. Wartime America was a golden age for Hollywood moviemakers.

JUNIOR COMMANDOS

"Save waste paper and scraps to help fight the Japs." The author of this book wrote that rhyme as a fourth-grader at the Blaine School in Chicago. It was 1944 and the teacher had asked the class to write a poem designed to spur the war effort. The attempt won first prize and the teacher wrote the poem boldly on the blackboard for all the class to see.

Kids and the War

The massive war effort swept up all Americans, including children. Kids hated the enemy with a mindless fury. In some neighborhoods, it was a custom for small children to destroy a toy—even if it was your favorite doll or model truck—if it was labeled "Made in Japan." At the local movie house boys and girls clapped and cheered as they watched newsreel films of German and Japanese cities burning under a rain of U.S. bombs. At school, kids followed maps showing Allied armies advancing on the enemy. Many children pasted war maps on their bedroom walls much the same way young people hang up pictures of rock stars today.

Kids lived with wartime fear. No one knew when his or her father, big brother, uncle, or nice neighbor who lived next door would be killed in combat. Tragically, some one hundred eighty-three thousand children lost their fathers during the war years. Still, it was an exciting time to grow up. Young minds found adventure and wonder in this war fought on faraway battlefronts.

In the summer of 1945, I went to a YMCA boys camp in Wisconsin. I remember Invasion Day, a war game played by all the campers. We dug foxholes. Teenage camp counselors wore surplus army helmets and played the role of enemy soldiers. Campers charged at the counselors using sticks as rifles. To us it was delirious fun. It did not occur to us that men on battlefields in Europe and Asia were at that very moment living in mud, trembling in terror, and dying horrible deaths. During Invasion Day we saw glory, not tragedy, in war.

The war left children to fend for themselves with little adult supervision. Fathers were away in the services and mothers were busy at factories. Day care centers were rare at that time. Miraculously, most of us avoided big trouble. Few toys were manufactured because factories were devoted to producing war goods. Therefore our games were the product of our imaginations. Most of us played war games with names we made up in the alley: "commandos," "guns," "combat." This author remembers playing "battle-ships" in a backyard mud puddle with another boy. We

SUDDENLY [AFTER PEARL HARBOR] YOU HAD A FLAGPOLE. AND A MARKER. NAMES WENT ON THE MARKER, GUYS FROM THE NEIGHBORHOOD WHO WERE KILLED. OUR NEIGHBORHOOD WAS DECIMATED . . . . THERE WAS THE CONSTANT IDEA THAT YOU HAD TO DO SOMETHING TO HELP . . . . [DURING AIR-RAID DRILLS] THE SIREN WOULD GO OFF AND EVERYBODY WOULD TURN OFF THE LIGHTS . . . . MY YOUNGER BROTHER AND I WOULD SIT THERE IN THIS ABSOLUTELY PITCH-BLACK APARTMENT. WE WERE AFRAID THAT IF WE DIDN'T, THE AIR-RAID WARDEN WOULD COME BY AND THE FBI WOULD COME AND TERRIBLE THINGS WOULD HAPPEN . . . . WE'D LISTEN TO THE RADIO EVERY NIGHT. MY FATHER WOULD TURN IT ON TO FIND OUT WHAT WAS HAPPENING. THE WAY A KID'S MIND COULD BE SHAPED BY THOSE . . . VOICES. THE WORLD WAS VERY SIMPLE. I SAW HITLER AND MUSSOLINI AND TOJO: THOSE WERE THE VILLAINS. WE WERE THE GOOD GUYS. AND THE RUSSIANS WERE THE GOOD GUYS TOO. THE WAR WAS ALWAYS BEING TALKED ABOUT [BY ADULTS]. EVERYBODY WAS A MILITARY STRATEGIST.[1]

Mike Royko was a nine-year-old Chicago boy when Pearl Harbor was attacked. He grew up to become a famous journalist. In 1984, he recalled his wartime childhood for an interview.

floated pieces of wood and puffed our cheeks making explosion sounds as our "battleships" slugged it out with their huge guns. Young artists scribbling on paper drew dogfights between fighter planes. Even a simple game of hide-and-seek played by the smallest kids took a military twist. When the seeker found the hider, he did not say, "You're it;" instead he said, "You're captured."

Early in the war children became sleuths in the spy mania rocking the country. Bands of farmboys in coastal New England roamed the shores armed with slingshots hoping to find German agents sneaking ashore in rubber craft. Along the California sea line, young patriots sought out Japanese infiltrators. I remember an encounter with a "spy" in my Chicago neighborhood. An Italian immigrant, new on the block, kept a horse in his garage. Horse-drawn wagons were common enough at the time. But this man had named his horse Mussolini, after the Fascist dictator of Italy. About a half dozen boys and girls debated if we should report the man to the FBI. We reasoned the horse with the odd name had to be linked to some sinister spy ring. It did not occur to us that the Italian man was perhaps an anti-Fascist and called his horse Mussolini in order to scorn the enemy leader. Finally the gang of us lost interest and wandered on home.

Comic-book heroes spurred the spy-catching mania. Comic books, which cost ten cents each, became a billion-dollar industry during the war. A popular monthly edition was called *Spy Smasher*. The comic-book detective Dick Tracy switched from hunting down criminals to capturing secret agents. Little Orphan Annie, the comic-strip heroine, was also dedicated to tracking down enemy agents. Captain Marvel battled a strange enemy invention: a super-intelligent worm called Mr. Mind. The greatest counterspy of all was Superman, the Man of Steel. Oddly, Superman failed the visual part of his army physical examination. Why? Because the Man of Steel's X-ray vision kept melting the eye charts.

Young people's movies, cartoons, and radio shows celebrated wartime heroics. War-action serials lasting fifteen minutes were popular at theaters. Each episode of the serial left the warrior in some death-defying position at the end. Thus young fans were compelled to return again next week and discover the hero's fate. *Don Winslow of the Navy* was a favorite wartime serial. A kids' radio show, *Terry and the Pirates*, dramatized the adventures of a fearless fighter squadron whose members rescued fellow pilots downed behind enemy lines. Everyone's favorite rabbit battled evil-looking, bucktoothed Japanese soldiers in the 1944 cartoon *Bugs Bunny Nips the Nips*. Kids shook with laughter as Bugs defeated the Japanese with the help of hand grenades disguised as ice-cream bars. Today the title of the cartoon would be considered vulgar and racist.

Boys became experts on military hardware. With one glance at a picture of a fighter plane a typical boy would exclaim, "That's a P-51 Mustang!" or, "Look at the twin fuselage, it's a P-38 Lightning!" Boys dreamed of one day piloting a fighter plane or driving a Sherman tank. Many harbored a secret hope that the war would last long enough for them to grow up, serve in uniform, and propel some fantastic military vehicle.

Pitching In

The demands of war meant that boys and girls had to work. It was the children's job, under the supervision of the mother, to tend the family victory garden. Boys and girls did housework to ease the burden of the mother who worked long hours in the local war plant. Girls made family meals with the aid of a government issued *Victory Cookbook*. The wartime cookbook emphasized vegetable and pasta dishes to replace scarce meat. Everyone, even small brothers and sisters, were required to eat every scrap of the kid-made meals. A government-sponsored "Clean Plate Program" said that wasting food was woefully unpatriotic. Rural boys and girls worked planting, bringing in harvests, and tending cows. Farm children earned the praise of the commander-in-chief in 1944, when President Franklin Roosevelt declared, "America's 1,700,000 organized junior farmers produced enough food to supply a million fighting men. They have set a standard for good citizen action."[2]

Helping in scrap drives was a primary task for home-front young people. The word *recycling* was not in use at the time, but scrap drives were in fact massive

Young people on the home front scouted for tin cans and old tires to help contribute during scrap drives.

recycling efforts. During scrap drives, teams of Boy Scouts and Girl Scouts tramped down alleys and side streets looking for tin cans and scrap metal. Members of scrap-drive teams proudly wore armbands. Adult scout leaders told the children that the metal in an old frying pan could be melted down and turned into a hand grenade. Kids were also told that a discarded shovel blade could be converted into a bayonet. A rusting old lawn mower was a real prize because it could be transformed into several artillery shells. Armed with this knowledge, scrap collectors became home-front soldiers. Some kids played imaginary games and sought out scrap as if they were marines on a jungle island hunting down enemy snipers. Perhaps the best scrappers belonged to an organization called Little Orphan Annie's Junior Commandos. The all-girl commandos cleaned alleys to the bone and brought in thousands of tons of scrap metal.

Paper, which was used to make packing material, was another vital substance for scrap drives. Every Wednesday was Paper Day in Chicago. Kids trudged to school carrying bundles of tied-up newspapers. The teacher measured each bundle with a ruler. The boy or girl who brought in the biggest one got to wear a gold-painted badge for the rest of the week. This author was privileged to wear the gold badge on two occasions.

Home-front recycling overlooked few items. In some communities a storekeeper refused to sell a customer a new tube of toothpaste unless he or she brought in the used one to be recycled. Taking waste meat fat to the butcher shop was another family project. Fats contained glycerine, which was made into gun powder. Shoppers carried the fats to the store in tin cans. Kids giggled at the hidden meaning in a sign that popped up in Chicago meat markets: "LADIES, PLEASE DON'T PUT YOUR FAT CANS ON THE RADIATOR."

Home-front boys and girls were often paid for their chores. However, their earnings were not to be wasted on candy and popcorn. A proper home-front youngster was expected to channel his or her money into the war effort. It was unrealistic to expect children to save their dimes and quarters until they could

Patriotic posters inspired home-front boys and girls to pitch in during the war. The message being delivered in this poster was to participate in scrap drives.

buy the cheapest bond, which cost $18.75. So, children bought "war stamps" for a dime each. These stamps (about the size of postage stamps) were pasted into a folder-type book called *My Victory Book*. The books were issued to every schoolchild. When the book was filled with 187 ten-cent stamps, the child marched it to the post office where the book was exchanged for a war bond worth $25 in ten years.

Most kids bought war stamps at school. Contests were held to see which classroom or school sold the greatest number of stamps. Teachers told their students that every ten-cent stamp they bought allowed the government to buy five machine-gun bullets.

Teenagers and the War

While young kids looked upon the war as an adventure, teenagers had far more serious views on the conflict. High school boys knew that shortly after graduation they would most likely go to basic training and then off to the battlefields. In fact, high schoolers did not have to wait until graduation to join up. With their parents' consent, seventeen-year-old boys could enlist. Each year thousands of teenage boys dropped out of school to join the services. With a critical labor shortage on the home front, teenagers were pressed into doing adult jobs. Local government officials simply looked the other way as companies violated the minimum-age work laws. Teenagers drove trucks, operated bulldozers, and ran heavy machinery in factories. By 1943, some 3 million teenage boys and girls worked full time. Almost half a million sixteen year olds toiled in war plants. Lured by high wages, an alarming number of teenagers left high school. After four years of war, high school attendance decreased by 1.25 million students.

Everything moved at a suddenly accelerated pace for young adults on the home front. Feeling the pressure, millions of young Americans rushed into marriage. The year 1942 saw a record number of requests for marriage licenses. Most of these marriage licenses were issued to young men who were about to enter basic training. By 1944, there were so many quicky marriages that the supply of gold wedding rings grew critically short.

Young couples tended to have babies soon after marriage. In 1943, more babies were born in the United States than in any other year since 1920. Many of these were "good-bye babies," infants born while the father was already in an army camp. The explosion in young married couples triggered the "baby boom" of the postwar years. The baby boom generation, born between 1946 and 1964, was the largest generation in U.S. history.

High school girls often had boyfriends or brothers in the armed forces. Consequently the girls battled loneliness, frustration, and fear. Teenage girls began to wear black rings on their fingers to symbolize their male friends in the services. For wartime fun the girls danced. Frequently they had to dance with each other since there were no boys available. In those days drugstores had soda fountains that served ice-cream treats such as Blackout Sundaes and Commando Sodas. At the far end of the soda fountain stood a juke-box. Selections on the jukebox cost five cents each to play. Putting a quarter in the slot gave a person a bonus sixth song. Drugstores and malt shops were favorite teen hangouts. Dancing to tunes on the jukebox was considered a lively way to pass a Saturday night.

Young girls frequently wore short white socks and were nicknamed bobby-soxers. The bobby-soxers had a hero in a skinny young singer from New Jersey named Frank Sinatra. Adult men scorned Sinatra because he was of draft age but did not serve due to punctured eardrums. A minor problem with eardrums seemed to be a feeble excuse to be deferred from service in the army. Sinatra's draft status did not diminish the passion felt by his female fans. Home-front girls tried to sneak into his hotel room and steal his used towels. Autograph-seekers tore at Sinatra's clothes, hoping to come away with a bow tie or a scrap of his shirt. Fans swooned and some fainted at his concerts. Sinatra's signature wartime song was "I'll Walk Alone." When that song played on jukeboxes, bobby-soxers cried out, "I'll walk with you, Frankie!"

A lack of adult supervision contributed to a shocking rise in juvenile delinquency among teenagers. In 1942, juvenile crime rose 8 percent among boys and an alarming 31 percent among girls. Yet violent teen behavior was minor compared to crime statistics compiled two generations later. Handguns and drugs had yet to become a large problem. Wartime teen crime usually took the form of vandalism and petty theft.

Out-of-wedlock teen pregnancy increased dramatically. Girls who were friendly—critics said too friendly—with servicemen were called Victory Girls. Boy rebels showed their defiance of authority by wearing a zoot suit, an outfit that featured baggy pants and a jacket with broad lapels. Young Mexican-American men favored the zoot suit. Soldiers and sailors believed the zoot suit craze was an unpatriotic display that aided the enemy. In 1943, sailors on shore leave in Los Angeles rioted, beating up those wearing zoot suits and ripping their clothing off their backs.

The vast majority of home-front teens remained law-abiding citizens during the war. High school boys could not help but hear the ticking of the clock as the war extended year by year. At age eighteen, boys faced the draft; and, after several months of training, they would face the enemy. Thus members of the high school class of 1942 landed on the bloody Pacific island of Tarawa in 1943. The class of 1943 stormed Europe on D-Day, 1944. The class of 1944 fought on Okinawa, an island off of Japan, and along the Rhine River on the border of Germany in 1945.

High schools kept lists of those graduates who were killed in action. The grim death lists were displayed in the school's main hallway near the athletic trophy case. Teachers looked at new names on the list and broke into tears as they remembered faces and personalities. They felt the deaths were a terrible waste.

American involvement in World War II lasted forty-four months (almost four years). The nation suffered more casualties—those killed and seriously wounded—during the last twelve months of the conflict than it had in the previous thirty-two months combined. Late 1944 and early 1945 saw glorious victories on the fighting fronts overseas. But during that period people on the home front grew war weary. Passion for the war effort diminished. Absenteeism in the factories rose. Americans went to bed every night and rose in the morning praying to God that the war would soon be over and their lives could return to normal.

WAR WEARINESS AND FINAL VICTORY

The Ultimate Symbol

Walk down any street in the home-front years and you were bound to see banners hanging in the windows of houses and apartments. The typical banner was a blue star against a field of white. Each blue star meant the household had a family member serving on active duty. Since one in five wartime families had a man or woman in the services, blue star banners were a common sight. Many banners had two, three, or even four blue stars. A banner on a White House window bore four stars. The stars represented the four Roosevelt sons, all of whom served in the armed forces.

Less common was a white banner with a gold star in the center. When a person saw a gold star he or she stopped, bowed his or her head, and said a silent prayer. A gold star meant that that household had lost a family member in the war. The gold star symbolized the war's ultimate tragedy. A young girl named Dianne Price described the effect a wartime death had on her family:

> After Uncle Eddy was killed, I remember a blue star was changed to gold. Grandma was never the same after that. My uncle's young wife was a basket case for a long time. My mother, who was trying to buoy everyone else up, almost had a nervous breakdown. For myself, I hated the war now. I had seen, first hand, how bad it could hurt.[1]

The nation's most famous gold-star family was the Sullivans of Waterloo, Iowa. Five Sullivan brothers joined the navy shortly after Pearl Harbor. They asked permission to serve on the same ship, and the navy granted their request. All five Sullivan boys were killed along with seven hundred of their shipmates when their cruiser, the *Juneau*, was sunk in battle off the island of Guadalcanal. A 1944 movie, *The Fighting Sullivans*, was produced honoring the family. The Sullivan parents

the five Sullivan brothers
'missing in action' off the Solomons

THEY DID THEIR PART

All five Sullivan sons were killed in action during the war. Their cruiser Juneau *was sunk in battle.*

were hailed as models of home-front courage, but it is impossible to gauge the scope of their suffering.

Triumphs and Setbacks

In early June 1944, church bells rang in home-front towns and cities. Motorists blew their car horns. High school bands assembled on the football field and played patriotic music. Home-front people celebrated a government announcement that on June 6 Allied forces launched the long-awaited invasion of France. This was D-Day, the sensational turning point in the war. Led by American General Dwight Eisenhower, U.S., British, Canadian, and Free French forces stormed ashore along the coast of France at Normandy to fight the occupying German forces. D-Day, the American public believed, was a giant step on the long road to victory.

Initially it seemed as though the German Army was on the verge of defeat. After a stubborn six-week battle near Normandy, Allied forces broke through German lines and began to race across France. The offensive was so successful that some allied leaders speculated that the war in Europe would be over by Christmas 1944. Many home-front families actually planned Christmas celebrations for their returning warriors. Then German resistance stiffened along the Rhine River. On December 16, the German Army struck with a massive counterattack. What the Americans called the Battle of the Bulge began. In 1944, home-front citizens suffered through another Christmas with their men far away.

On the other side of the world the pattern was similar. Island by island the Japanese gave ground. In America, the concept was called "island hopping," using tiny Pacific islands as stepping-stones to Japan. The Philippines were liberated in early 1945. Formations of huge B-29 bombers took off from island bases to smash Japanese cities. But the Japanese, always tough fighters, grew even more fanatical as American forces advanced. Off the island of Okinawa in 1945, Japanese flyers employed large-scale kamikaze, or suicide, attacks. Pilots, accepting death, dove their aircraft directly into U.S. ships as if the planes were human-driven guided missiles.

In February 1945, U.S. Marines assaulted Iwo Jima, an ugly rock of an island that lay 750 miles south of Tokyo, Japan. During twenty-six days of savage fighting, some six thousand marines were killed. It was the bloodiest battle the marines had fought so far in

This dramatic combat photo taken in February 1945 records a group of marines raising the American flag at Iwo Jima. It helped to inspire a war-weary American public.

the war. But from Iwo Jima a dramatic photograph boosted home-front moral. The picture, taken by Joe Rosenthal of the Associated Press, showed a group of marines raising the American flag over the island's highest mountain. The photo appeared on front pages in dozens of American newspapers. Today, the flag raising at Iwo Jima is hailed as the most exciting picture taken in World War II.

On March 29, 1945, President Franklin Roosevelt enjoyed a brief vacation at his retreat in Warm Springs, Georgia. Suddenly he said, "I have a terrific headache." Then he collapsed. Roosevelt died a few hours later at the age of sixty-three. People close to the president knew that war worries had taken their toll on his health. Roosevelt had lost weight, and dark circles had appeared surrounding his eyes. Despite his frail appearance, the American public refused to believe their leader was near death. Roosevelt was the anchor that kept the nation steady. For twelve years he led his nation through the Great Depression and through the most costly war in history. Now, when that war neared a conclusion, the shock of his death was overpowering. Americans wept on the streets. Even the president's political enemies—and he had many—shed tears.

In Germany, Adolf Hitler rejoiced over the American president's sudden death. Hitler believed that America, suddenly without its leader, would falter in war. Despite Hitler's confidence, Germany's enemies were closing in from both sides, crushing the country in the jaws of a vice. On April 22, 1945,

Soviet troops entered Berlin. Three days later American and Soviet forces met on German soil. On April 30, Adolf Hitler swallowed poison and shot himself. With their leader dead, German officials surrendered to the Allies on May 7, 1945.

Adolf Hitler had promised the German people a government so strong it would last one thousand years. Just four years earlier Hitler and the Germans were masters over most of Europe. Now Germany was a shattered nation. More than 4.5 million Germans (one million of whom were civilians) were dead, and the country was occupied by foreign armies.

At home, people celebrated V-E Day, Victory Day in Europe. The celebrations were low-key. Everyone was painfully aware that the Japanese, whose warriors seemed to prefer suicide to surrender, had to be conquered. What frightful losses could the Americans expect when invading the home island of Japan?

Manhattan Project and Final Victory

Moments after Franklin Roosevelt's death, the little-known vice president, Harry Truman, was sworn in as president. It was only then that Truman learned of the Manhattan Project, an effort so secret that not even the next president-in-line was told of its existence.

The Manhattan Project was the code name for the massive American attempt to create a powerful weapon called an atomic bomb. Building the bomb was one of the most ambitious scientific enterprises ever launched by the United States. Work was

In this photograph, a New York City neighborhood celebrates final victory after the nation suffered through more than three and a half years of war.

conducted in thirty-seven installations spread over thirteen different states. More than one hundred twenty thousand men and women worked on the project, but only a handful knew they were building an atomic weapon.

On August 6, 1945, an atomic bomb was dropped on the city of Hiroshima, Japan, by a high-flying B-29 bomber. One aircraft. One bomb. And the world was never the same place again. A dazzling ball of orange burst over the city. Temperatures inside that ball were three times greater than on the surface of the sun. People directly below the blast vaporized in the time it takes to blink an eye. Those farther away suffered agonizing burns that tortured them for the rest of their lives. At least eighty thousand people in Hiroshima died the first day. No one knows the number who died later of wounds and radiation sickness caused by this devastating weapon.

After Hiroshima, events in the Pacific moved with startling speed. On August 8, the Soviet Union declared war on Japan. The next day a second atomic bomb was dropped by a U.S. bomber on the Japanese city of Nagasaki. On August 14, Japan agreed to surrender terms with the United States.

V-J Day! Victory over Japan! The war was over! The home front exploded in joy. Americans rushed downtown, hearing the music and following the crowds. Everyone longed to be with others and join the nationwide party. Perfect strangers embraced and danced together on the streets. V-J Day was the conclusion of a terrible war that had lasted more than three and a half years. In that time Americans had built the greatest war machine in history. Now the citizens celebrated victory and peace on earth. And the real triumph would come in the ensuing months as thousands of soldiers and sailors returned home from overseas.

Thanks to the efforts of home-front citizens, the United States emerged from World War II as the most powerful nation in the world. America was the only major combatant that had not been bombed, nor had it suffered the destruction of combat on its soil. No people enjoyed greater wealth and stability. But the home front's most significant creation, the atomic bomb, brought forth a cloud of fear that now hung over the earth. The home-front experience had changed the country—and the world—forever.

★ TIMELINE ★

1939—*September 1*: Germany invades Poland; historians consider this invasion to be the start of World War II.

September 3: Britain and France declare war on Germany.

September 5: The United States declares its neutrality in the war.

1940—*June 11*: The U.S. Congress passes a bill authorizing $1.5 billion for a shipbuilding program.

June 22: France surrenders to Germany.

September 22: Japan attacks French Indochina.

October 16: Draft registration begins in the United States; all men age eighteen must register for the draft.

1941—*June 22*: Germany invades Russia.

December 7: Japan bombs Pearl Harbor.

December 8: The United States declares war on Japan.

December 11: Germany and Italy declare war on the United States.

1942—*February 22*: President Roosevelt signs Executive Order 9066, which relocates all people of Japanese heritage from western states of the United States.

April 9: Remaining U.S. forces on the Philippines surrender to the Japanese.

April 18: U.S. planes led by Colonel James Doolittle bomb Japan; the raid is cheered by home-front people.

June 4–6: The U.S. Navy inflicts severe losses on the Japanese fleet at the Battle of Midway.

June 15–30: Americans from every state participate in a giant scrap-rubber drive, the first of many such scrap drives conducted on the home front.

August 7: American Marines land on Guadalcanal, launching the first U.S. ground offensive in the Pacific.

November 7: American Army units land in North Africa.

November 28: Coffee rationing is put into effect.

December 1: Gasoline rationing is ordered for every state.

1943—*April 8*: President Roosevelt freezes prices and wages in an effort to curb home-front inflation.

June 1: More than five hundred thousand coal miners go on strike; The strike is settled before it hampers U.S. war production.

June 9: A "pay-as-you-go" tax system begins as a wartime emergency measure; Taxes are now deducted from workers' paychecks.

June 20–22: Race riots rock Detroit and spread to other cities; African Americans cite housing discrimination for the disturbances in Detroit.

July 10: Allied forces land on Sicily.

September 8: Italy drops out of the war.

November 6: Russian troops recapture the city of Kiev.

November 20: Marines invade the Pacific island of Tarawa.

1944—*June 4*: U.S. soldiers enter Rome, Italy.

June 6: D day, Allied forces invade Normandy in France; Home-front Americans celebrate the invasion.

June 15: American Marines and Army units invade Saipan in the Pacific.

July 21: The Democratic party, meeting in Chicago, nominates Franklin Roosevelt as its presidential candidate.

August 14: In a move to ease home-front shortages, Congress authorizes the limited manufacture of kitchen appliances such as kitchen stoves and refrigerators.

August 25: Allies liberate Paris, France.

November 7: Franklin Roosevelt is elected to a fourth term as president.

November 24: Huge B-29 bombers begin massive air raids on Japan.

December 16: German troops launch the Battle of the Bulge.

1945—*January 9*: American Army units land at Luzon in the Philippines.

February 19: Marines land at Iwo Jima; Days after the invasion, a photographer snaps the heroic flag-raising photo that boosts home-front morale.

March 7: The U.S. Army crosses the Rhine River and enters Germany.

April 1: U.S. forces invade Okinawa Island, some 350 miles from Japan.

April 12: Franklin Roosevelt dies; Harry Truman is sworn in as president.

April 22: Russian soldiers enter the suburbs of Berlin.

April 30: Adolf Hitler commits suicide in his Berlin bunker.

May 5: A woman and five children are killed near Lakeview, Oregon, by a "balloon bomb" launched days earlier from Japan; they are the only American civilian bombing casualties of World War II.

May 7: German forces surrender to the Allies.

August 6: A U.S. B-29 drops an atomic bomb on Hiroshima, Japan.

August 8: Russia declares war on Japan.

August 9: Atomic bomb dropped on Nagasaki.

August 14: Japan announces it will surrender to the United States.

September 2: Millions of home-front Americans throw parties as Japan officially surrenders and World War II comes to a close.

★ CHAPTER NOTES ★

Chapter 2. Remember Pearl Harbor

1. William Manchester, *The Glory and the Dream* (Boston: Little Brown, 1973), p. 253.

2. *Annals of America*, vol. 16 (Chicago: Encyclopedia Britannica, Inc., 1976), p. 103.

Chapter 3. A Nation in the Grip of Fear

1. Richard Polenberg, ed., *America at War: The Home Front, 1941–1945* (Englewood Cliffs, N.J.: Prentice Hall, 1968), p. 7.

2. Ronald H. Bailey, *The Home Front: U.S.A.* (Chicago: Time-Life Books, 1978), p. 12.

3. *Life* magazine, December 22, 1941.

4. William Manchester, *The Glory and the Dream* (Boston: Little Brown, 1973), p. 298.

5. Ibid.

6. Mark Jonathan Harris, Franklin D. Mitchell, Steven J. Schechter, *The Homefront: America During World War II* (New York: G. P. Putnam's Sons, 1984), p. 111.

7. Yukio Uchida, *Desert Exile: The Uprooting of a Japanese-American Family* (Seattle: University of Washington Press, 1982), p. 96.

8. Bailey, p. 30.

Chapter 4. The War Effort

1. *Annals of America*, vol. 16 (Chicago: Encyclopedia Britannica, Inc., 1976), p. 105.

2. Mark Jonathan Harris, Franklin D. Mitchell, Steven J. Schechter, *The Homefront: America During World War II* (New York: G. P. Putnam's Sons, 1984), p. 48.

3. Ibid., p. 105.

4. Nancy J. Skarmeas, *Victory* (Nashville, Tenn.: Ideals Publications, Inc., 1995), p. 10.

5. Tom Brokaw, *The Greatest Generation Speaks* (New York: Random House, 1999), p. 14.

6. *Annals of America*, vol. 16, p. 128.

7. David M. Kennedy, *Freedom from Fear: The American People in Depression and War, 1929–1945* (New York: Oxford University Press, 1999), p. 653.

8. Winston Churchill, "Lord Mayor's Day Speech," November 10, 1942.

Chapter 5. The Arsenal of Democracy

1. William Manchester, *The Glory and the Dream* (Boston: Little Brown, 1973), p. 296.

2. Donald I. Rogers, *Since You Went Away* (New Rochelle, N.Y.: Arlington House, 1973), p. 145.

Chapter 6. An Army of Workers

1. Mark Jonathan Harris, Franklin D. Mitchell, Steven J. Schechter, *The Homefront: America During World War II* (New York: G. P. Putnam's Sons, 1984), p. 121.

2. David M. Kennedy, *Freedom from Fear: The American People in Depression and War, 1929–1945* (New York: Oxford University Press, 1999), p. 644.

3. Ibid., p. 643.

4. Richard Polenberg, ed., *America at War: The Home Front, 1941–1945* (Englewood Cliffs, N.J.: Prentice Hall, 1968), p. 135.

5. Harris, Mitchell, and Schechter, p. 204.

6. Polenberg, p. 131.

7. Ibid., p. 125.

8. Kennedy, p. 767.

9. "U.S. at War," *Time*, June 28, 1943, p. 19.

Chapter 7. *V* is for *Victory*

1. Richard Polenberg, ed., *America at War: The Home Front, 1941–1945* (Englewood Cliffs, N.J.: Prentice Hall, 1968), p. 11.

2. Paul Fussell, *Wartime: Understanding and Behavior in the Second World War* (New York: Oxford University Press, 1989), p. 197.

3. Bob Hope with Melville Shavelson, *Don't Shoot, It's Only Me* (New York: G. P. Putnam's Sons, 1990), p. 84.

4. Mary Livingston Benny and Hilliard Marks, *Jack Benny* (New York: Doubleday, 1978), p. 154.

5. Gabe Essoe, *Tarzan of the Movies* (New York: The Citadel Press, 1968), p. 115.

6. Roger Manvell, *Films and the Second World War* (New York: A. S. Barns and Co., 1974), pp. 188–189.

Chapter 8. Junior Commandos

1. Studs Terkel, *The Good War* (New York: Pantheon, 1984), pp. 135–136.

2. *National Geographic*, July 1944, p. XIV.

Chapter 9. War Weariness and Final Victory

1. James W. Wensyel, "Homefront," *American History*, June 1995, p. 44.

★ FURTHER READING ★

Collier, Christopher, and James Lincoln Collier. *The United States in World War II*. Tarrytown, N.Y.: Marshall Cavendish Corporation, 2001.

Colman, Penny. *Rosie the Riveter: Women Working on the Homefront in World War II*. New York: Crown Publishing Group, 1998.

Krull, Kathleen. *V Is for Victory*. New York: Alfred A. Knopf, 1995.

Sullivan, George. *The Day Pearl Harbor Was Bombed: A Photo History of World War II*. New York: Scholastic, 1991.

Uchida, Yukio. *Desert Exile: The Uprooting of a Japanese-American Family*. Seattle: University of Washington Press, 1982.

Whitman, Sylvia. *Uncle Sam Wants You: Military Men and Women of World War II*. Minneapolis: Lerner Books, 1993.

———. *V Is for Victory: The American Home Front During World War II*. Minneapolis: Lerner Books, 1993.

★ INTERNET ADDRESSES ★

Library of Congress. "America from the Great Depression to World War II: Photographs from the FSA-OWI, 1935–1945." *American Memory Collection*. 1998. <http://memory.loc.gov/ammem/fsowhome.html>.

Rutgers, The State University of New Jersey, History Department. *The Rutgers Oral History Archives of World War II Web Archive*. February 21, 2002. <http://fas-history.rutgers .edu/oralhistory/>.

ThinkQuest. *World War II: The Homefront*. 1998. <http://library .thinkquest.org/15511/>.

★ INDEX ★